BIBLE
MANUSCRIPTS
1400 Years of Scribes and Scripture

BIBLE
MANUSCRIPTS

1400 Years of Scribes and Scripture

Scot McKendrick and Kathleen Doyle

The British Library

NOTE TO THE READER

The colour plates on pp. 14–156 are arranged broadly in chronological order. The captions accompanying the plates are divided into two parts: the shorter provides specific details of the manuscript reproduced, while the longer offers a brief commentary on its significance within the history of the Bible. Included in the short caption is an identification of the biblical text and/or subject of the illumination and the language in which it is written, the name or identification of the manuscript in italics, an attribution of origin and date, measurements of a whole page in millimetres and the full British Library manuscript reference. Where a plate reproduces the actual size of a manuscript, this is noted. For plates reproducing only or mainly an image, no biblical reference is given, unless the image is contained in an initial, border or margin. A biblical reference without a chapter or verse number indicates respectively the beginning of a book or chapter. Biblical references are to modern chapter numbers, with the Vulgate numbering and book titles following in brackets afterwards. Biblical quotations are from the New International Version.

ABOVE Elders of the Apocalypse
The Silos Apocalypse
Silos, Spain
1109
Add. MS 11695, f. 83 (detail)

HALF-TITLE PAGE John seated
The Stavelot Bible
Stavelot, near Liège, southern Netherlands
1093–97
Add. MS 28107, f. 201 (detail)

TITLE PAGE The Last Supper
Gospel Lectionary
Hirsau?, southern Germany
c. 1100
Egerton MS 809, f. 17 (detail)

FRONT JACKET Evangelist portrait of Matthew
The Arnstein Bible
Arnstein, near Koblenz, Germany
c. 1172
Harley MS 2799, f. 155 (detail)

BACK JACKET The Seven Gifts of the Holy Spirit
La Charité Psalter
La Charité-sur-Loire, France
last quarter of 12th century
Harley MS 2895, f. 83 (detail)

Contents

Introduction

The Christian Bible has a unique place in the history of the book. Before the advent of printing in the West no text was so frequently revered by the faithful, laboured over by scribes and illuminators, studied by scholars and coveted by the rich and powerful. Surviving handwritten copies, or manuscripts, of the Bible include the finest specimens of their times of the arts of calligraphy, illumination and book-production; some, although more humble in outward appearance, preserve unique or significant readings which shape the modern text of the Bible. Many Bibles were written and decorated by monks and other members of religious communities, as part of their life of sacrificial praise to God, others by professional craftsmen for lay readers. Some were intended for personal study and meditation, some for reading and as a physical symbol of the Word of God within a Christian community, and others for evangelizing or for missionary purposes. Bible manuscripts thereby reveal not only the remarkable history of an extraordinarily influential text, but also map the development of the book before the invention of printing.

The Bible that we know today is different in many respects from that known to Christians during the 1500 years in which the text was copied by hand. For, whereas the biblical text may be essentially the same now as then, the format in which that text is now presented is much changed. A typical modern Bible is a single volume of modest proportions, somewhat austere in its unadorned and dense presentation of printed text. Divisions in the text are clearly marked and referenced according to a standardized system of numbering by chapter and verse, allowing easy comparison between different copies, regardless of version or language. Wherever it is available today, the Bible is aimed at the widest possible readership, written in the language spoken in the relevant region or country and distributed at a price affordable to people living there. What follows highlights some of the individual features of

OPPOSITE Annunciation
Four Gospels
Echternach, near Trier, Germany,
middle of 11th century
255 x 190 mm
Harley MS 2821, f. 22

OVERLEAF Centres of Christianity
from the 2nd to 16th centuries.

Bible manuscripts and the ways in which they differ from modern Bibles.

Handwritten copies of parts of what we know as the New Testament apparently began to circulate amongst the faithful in the late 1st century. In content these copies built on the apostolic letters written by Paul to specific early Christian communities and on stories of the life and teaching of Jesus passed by word of mouth, committed to memory amongst the earliest Christians and written down by the Evangelists. In format they were rather humble copies, similar in size to modern pocket paperbacks and comprising mainly single books of the Bible (fig. 4) and only occasionally small groups of books such as the Four Gospels. Although typical of Graeco-Roman books in their use of papyrus for writing material, early Christian books were distinctive in their use of the codex, or book form, rather than a roll format. In this respect they form part of a critical transition in the history of the book when the traditional format of the roll, used by all literate cultures in the Mediterranean world for many millennia, was replaced by the book format. Although scrolled text on personal computers and other electronic devices has brought about a return of the roll format, the book format continues to shape much of the text that we read today.

Whereas their format is familiar, the content of some of the earliest surviving Christian books is unfamiliar. Several written accounts of the teaching of Jesus that differ from the texts of the New Testament are preserved to this day in unique or very rare copies. Some, such as the Unknown Gospel (fig. 3) or the Gospel of Thomas (fig. 5), echo the contents, and even wording, of the Four Gospels in modern Bibles; others, such as the recently discovered and published Gospel of Judas, present sensationally different versions of the story. Paul's corpus of letters was extended to include a third letter to the Corinthians. Even familiar texts appear in unfamiliar order: the Gospels, for example, could begin with Matthew, but then continue with John, Luke and Mark.

More familiar, in both format and content, to modern readers is *Codex Sinaiticus* (fig. 7). Originally intended to contain the whole of the Old and New Testaments, this massive volume aimed to establish beyond dispute which texts formed part of what is called the canon of scripture. The overall contents of this manuscript signalled what was approved by the Christian Church as newly authorized by

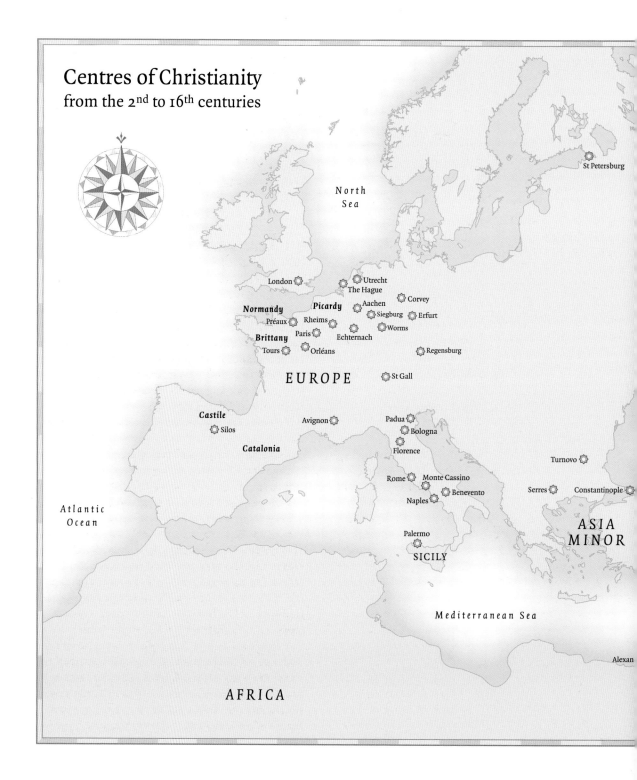

Centres of Christianity
from the 2nd to 16th centuries

St Petersburg

North Sea

London
Utrecht
The Hague
Normandy **Picardy** Aachen Corvey
Préaux Rheims Siegburg Erfurt
Paris Worms
Brittany Echternach
Tours Orléans Regensburg

EUROPE St Gall

Castile
Silos
Avignon Padua
Catalonia Bologna
Florence
Turnovo
Rome Monte Cassino
Serres Constantinople
Naples Benevento

Atlantic Ocean

ASIA MINOR

Palermo
SICILY

Mediterranean Sea

Alexan

AFRICA

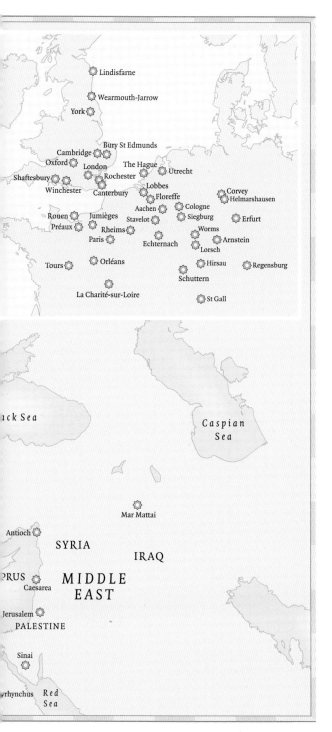

the Emperor Constantine the Great in the first half of
the 4th century. After so many years of persecution by
the Roman authorities and threats of internal schism,
Christians at last had physically, as well as in principle, a
single book of scripture. To achieve this significant step
in the history of the Bible, book technology had also to
develop further: papyrus was replaced by the more robust
parchment, and binding structures became more complex
and resilient. More formal presentation of the text necessi-
tated greater care in the layout of each page of text, finer
calligraphy and more refined articulation of the text.
Such advances in book technology enabled the canon of
scripture to be captured in its further recensions over
succeeding centuries.

In the 5th century, Christian books of scripture
developed to include significant decoration, incorporating
early Christian symbols and images employed in painting
and other modes of artistic and religious expression. Thus,
in *Codex Alexandrinus* (fig. 8) we find some of the earliest
examples of significant book decoration marking the end
of each of the biblical books. In the Cotton Genesis (fig. 9)
we encounter one of the most extended campaigns of
illustration for a single book of the Bible. In their different
ways, both manuscripts were harbingers of the distinctive
artistic splendour and pictorial richness of so many later
manuscripts of the Bible. Within that later tradition decoration brought a fitting beauty to scripture, with individual
words transmuted by lavish calligraphy.

For a thousand years images were used in manuscripts
to enhance the structure, authority, narrative and teaching
of biblical text. An illuminated portrait of an Evangelist
placed at the beginning of each of the Gospels in the most
lavish copies of the text emphasized the authority and
individuality of each Evangelist's message about Jesus.
An image inserted into the decorated first letter of a text,
such as that of Job and his family (fig. 63), facilitated quick
recognition of the identity of that text. Applied more exten-
sively, images provided visual commentaries on the text,
helping to transform copies of Jewish scripture into Christian books and to stress the precedents for the New Law of
Christianity in the Old Law of Judaism. Images could also
be used to instruct the literate on complex theological
matters. Moreover they could replace written text and instruct those to whom images spoke more directly than text
about the story of Jesus or the basic beliefs of the Christian

faith. Honoured rather than worshipped, images of all three persons of the Christian Trinity – Father, Son and Holy Spirit – became an acceptable and common feature of biblical manuscripts throughout the Christian world.

In parallel with the developments in format during the 4th and 5th centuries, the language of Bible manuscripts had also been changing. The earliest Christians had written their scriptures in Greek and adopted a Greek version of Jewish scripture known as the Septuagint. But, as the Christian faith spread to other regions and nations, so their scriptures were translated into other languages, beginning with those of the earliest converts and including Coptic, Syriac (fig. 91), Ethiopian and Armenian. With full papal authority, the early Christian scholar Jerome (figs 13, 24) also initiated a translation of the complete Bible into Latin, producing what, as the Vulgate (or common version), became the standard version of Christian scripture in western Europe for over one thousand years. During this same period all translations of the Bible into western vernacular languages were made from the Vulgate. Only the Reformation brought new translations of the entire Bible based on the original Hebrew and Greek texts (fig. 141). Ironically these translations were based on manuscripts that were inferior in quality to those employed by Jerome.

The large-format Bible, in one or several volumes, like *Codex Sinaiticus* and *Codex Alexandrinus*, was not, however, the most common form of Bible within the manuscript era. During these 1400 years, the most common book was not a complete Bible, but a portion of the Bible. This fact may seem strange to a modern owner of a Bible. Yet, frequency of use was a much stronger factor in determining what was produced in the era before printing when every word was the result of painstaking copying by hand and entailed significant labour or cost, or both. Matching the production of Bible manuscripts to their likely use thus resulted in the creation of thousands of copies of the most commonly used books of the Bible. Perhaps the most ubiquitous Christian book was the Four Gospels, either preserving the distinct sequence of each text or with selected passages re-ordered in line with the readings employed in the Church year to form a Lectionary. Also particularly numerous were Psalters, which were essentially copies of the Psalms structured to mirror their daily use in monastic liturgy. Since the Gospels and Psalms

formed central parts of Christian services from the earliest days, it was natural that copies of them were in high demand. For similar reasons, the Epistles in lectionary form were also common (figs 75, 119). Although never so popular as the Gospels, Psalms, or Epistles, the book of Revelation, or Apocalypse, also appeared in separate volumes, each time prompted by a particular interest in its distinctive and apocalyptic vision of the future (figs 60, 101–2, 111–12). Like several other individual books of the Bible, its text was most often copied in conjunction with, and in the same volume as, a commentary explaining it. Copies of the Gospels, Epistles or Psalms that include the elaborate commentaries known as the *Glossa ordinaria* and *Magna glossatura* are some of the most common books of the Latin Bible to survive from the 12th century (figs 84, 87).

When, therefore, we encounter manuscripts containing the whole Bible, we should seek to understand the particular reasons behind their production. The huge one-volume Bibles, or pandects, produced in Northumbria under Abbot Ceolfrid (fig. 17) and at Tours under the Emperor Charlemagne and his successors (fig. 21), came into being as much to progress the political ambitions of their sponsors as to preserve the biblical text. Confronted with such vast monuments of high artistic skill, cultural sophistication, power and wealth, who could fail to be impressed and stand in awe of their creators? Similarly, the enormous Romanesque Bibles (figs 63, 67, 79–82) stand testament to the power and wealth of the great monastic houses for which they were produced, as well as to the central importance of scripture to the lives of the monks. Small Bibles require an entirely different explanation. The so-called pocket Bibles produced in the 13th century (figs 97–98) appear to have arisen to address the specific context of preaching and the evangelistic mission of the friars. In this context a complete, portable text of the Bible was a great advantage. As in the case of modern Bibles, that crucial portability was achieved through the use of tiny script and pages of lightweight, very thin material. Strikingly, all such traditions of complete Bible production arise only in western Europe and have no parallel in, for example, the Byzantine empire.

Similarly, whereas today we take for granted the comprehensive system of biblical reference by chapter and verse, this system was not in use for most of the manuscript era. Numbering parts of the Gospels was introduced at an early date and further exploited by the Christian writer Eusebius (d. 340), whose ten Canon tables employed the numbering system attributed to Ammonius of Alexandria to allow comparison of similar episodes in the four texts (figs 1–2, 28, 43, 47). The Psalms were also individually numbered early on. Other systems of dividing biblical texts either by headings or numbers were used in individual copies or by individual commentators, but were of very limited use for comparison given the varying methods employed. Only in the early 13th century did teachers and students of the university of Paris begin to use the standardized system of chapter numbering that we now use. Often ascribed to Stephen Langton (d. 1228), Archbishop of Canterbury, this means of referencing biblical text remained the principal one until the introduction of verse numbers by Robert Estienne for his edition of the Bible in French, printed at Geneva in 1553.

Like modern printed Bibles, manuscript Bibles were used for many different purposes. Shaped to fit easily into the palm of a hand, small manuscripts enabled private reading, devotion or study wherever it was required, as well as preaching to others in various formal and informal settings. Such portability also established a direct connection between an individual and the biblical text and sometimes encouraged the owner of a manuscript Bible to believe in the talismanic power of his book (fig. 15). Larger volumes, like modern lectern Bibles, enabled easy reading in the communal setting of mealtimes, teaching and the liturgy. Embellished on the outside with precious metal and jewels, their remarkable materiality enhanced the faithful's sense of the presence of God, complementing that brought to them in the bread and wine of the Mass. According to one scribe, the manuscript of the Gospels that he wrote (fig. 122) was created 'not simply for the outward beauty of its decoration … [but] primarily to express the inner Divine Word, the revelation and the sacred vision'.

Unlike a printed Bible, every manuscript Bible is a unique artefact. One volume might be produced by a believer for his own use, another by a monk wishing to benefit the religious or secular life of his community, and yet another by a team of professional artists and scribes seeking to keep their families housed and fed. Yet, each was the product of particular, skilled artisans and the result of a unique set of circumstances. Although always copied from another manuscript, each volume constitutes a partic-

ular solution to the challenges of making a book; one copy differed from another copy in, for example, the handwriting, the version of the text, and the extent and character of any decoration or illustration. In an era of mass production we may find it difficult to appreciate fully the labour and skill involved in every hand-written book. Moreover, since very few manuscripts preserve details of the exact circumstances of their production, much that we know about them is dependent on scholarly expertise and judgment. Yet, manuscript Bibles remain a remarkable source of direct contact with some of the most talented craftsmen of their times, who despite their frequent anonymity have the power to speak across the centuries to our current generation.

Such in outline is the distinctive character of the manuscript tradition of the Bible. To illustrate that tradition we have had the great privilege of selecting items from the manuscript holdings of the British Library. Incomparable in its depth and breadth, this world-famous collection preserves major landmarks of Bible production created over 1400 years, ranging from the earliest days of the Christian Church in the eastern Mediterranean to the time of the Byzantine and Carolingian empires, the high and later middle ages in western and eastern Europe, the continuing eastern Church under Islam, and the early days of the western Reformation. Through reproductions of some 140 pages selected from these manuscripts, this book seeks to outline how the Christian Bible was preserved and passed down between the era of the Emperors Trajan and Hadrian and that of Queen Elizabeth I.

Scot McKendrick

RIGHT Portrait of Mark
Bible, Bologna, Italy
last quarter of 13th century
Add. MS 18720, Vol. 2, f. 422v (detail)

verbū. Et uerbū erat apud dm̄. Et d̄s erat
uerbū. Hoc erat inprincipio apud deum.
Omnia p̄ipsū facta s̄t. & sine ipso factū est
nichil. Quod factū est. inipso uita erat.
Et uita erat lux hominū. & lux in tenebꝭs
lucet. et tenebre eam non cōprehendert.
fuit homo missus a d̄o. cui nomen erat io
hannes. Hic uenit in testimoniū ut testi
moniū p̄hiberet de lumine. ut om̄s cre
derent p̄illū. Non erat ille lux. sed ut tes
timoniū p̄hiberet de lumine. Erat lux
uera. que illuminat omnē hominē ue
nientē in hunc mundū. In mundo erat
& mundus p̄ipsū factus est. & mundus
eū non cognouit. In p̄pria uenit. & sui
eū non recepunt. Quotq̄t aū recepunt eū

Io. i. III.
☩. i.
lu. xviii.

Io. ii. III.
☩. vii.
lu. vi.

Io. iii. III.
☩. i.
r. xviii.

Io. iiii. III.
sol? x

THE MANUSCRIPTS

1–2 Canon tables, in Greek
The Golden Canon Tables
Constantinople ?
6th or 7th century
210 x 170 mm (each)
Add. MS 5111, ff. 10–11

These two leaves are all that is known to survive of an extraordinary deluxe manuscript of the Four Gospels. Written on gold, and painted with great skill, they are arguably the most splendid fragments to survive from the early Christian period. Their text is part of the Canon tables, a concordance (or cross-referencing system) that enables the reader to trace similar passages in different Gospels, together with the preface explaining how to use them. The columnar layout presented artistic opportunities for embellishment – most commonly, an

architectural frame that was drawn around the text. Here the frames are augmented by medallion busts of the Apostles. On the left is part of the preface by Eusebius, Bishop of Caesarea (315–c.338/9), the compiler of the tables. On the right are Canon tables eight to ten, identifying the parallels between Matthew and Mark, and between Luke and John, and passages that occur in only one Gospel. An efficient tool for study and comparison, the tables in their decorated frames also served as an elegant introduction or 'gateway' to the Gospels.

3 Fragments of an unknown gospel, in Greek
The Egerton Gospel
Egypt
1st half of 2nd century
120 x 100 mm and 115 x 90 mm
(the larger fragments)
Egerton Papyrus 2 recto

These fragments from a papyrus codex, or booklet, form parts of one of the two earliest surviving Christian books. Their text relates several of the same stories as found in the Four canonical Gospels, and in a similar narrative manner. The text is a very early elaboration on the Gospel story that includes a mysterious passage without parallel in the canonical Gospels. In the lower fragment the text corresponds with passages in chapters 8 and 10 of John's Gospel.

Many early Christian texts were written in booklets rather than on rolls, which was the more typical format in the ancient world. That this papyrus was part of such a booklet is clear from the vertical blank space in the middle of it, where the page was originally folded. The combination of the first chapter of John (on the left) and of chapter 20 (on the right) also identifies the text as preserving part of a small book of the Gospel of John.

4 Fragments of John 1 and 20, in Greek
Fragment of a Greek codex
Egypt
3rd century
210 x 75 mm
Papyrus 782

5 Preface and Sayings of Jesus, in Greek
Gospel of Thomas
Egypt
3rd century
245 x 80 mm
Papyrus 1531 verso

This fragment from a papyrus roll preserves the beginning of a collection of Christ's sayings known as the Gospel of Thomas. Unlike the canonical Gospels, the Gospel of Thomas does not narrate the life of Jesus, but comprises a collection of 114 of his sayings. The start of each saying is here marked by a horizontal line, or *paragraphus*. The abbreviated form (IHC) of the name 'Jesus' is legible 7 and 16 lines up from the lower edge.

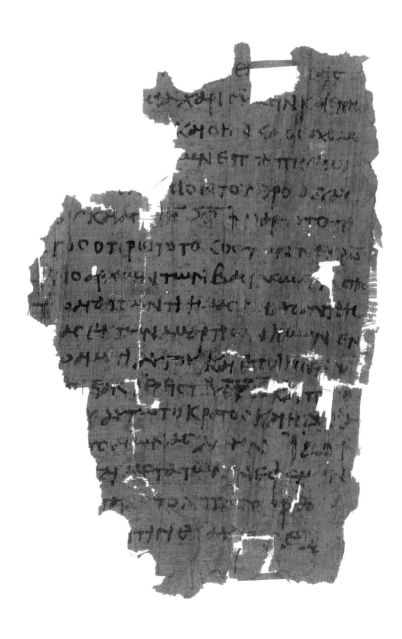

Unearthed in the rubbish tips of the ancient city of Oxyrhynchus, this fragment from a papyrus roll is one of the earliest witnesses of the book of Revelation. It was written by an unidentified early Christian living in Middle Egypt, who re-used a papyrus roll of the Greek text of the book of Exodus and wrote on its blank reverse. It is possible that this scribe was a Jewish convert to Christianity, who had available a family copy of Exodus.

6 Revelation 1:4–7, in Greek
Fragment of a Greek roll
Egypt
3rd or 4th century
150 x 100 mm (shown at actual size)
Papyrus 2053 verso

7 End of John, in Greek
Codex Sinaiticus
Egypt or Palestine ?
4th century
380 x 345 mm
Add. MS 43725, f. 260

Codex Sinaiticus, or the book from Sinai, is justly famous for its preservation of the earliest surviving copy of the complete New Testament and as the earliest and best witness for some books of the Old Testament. Its pages are remarkable both for the layout of the text in four columns, and the density of later corrections to the main text. As one of the earliest luxury codices to survive in large part, it also forms one of the most important landmarks in the history of the book.

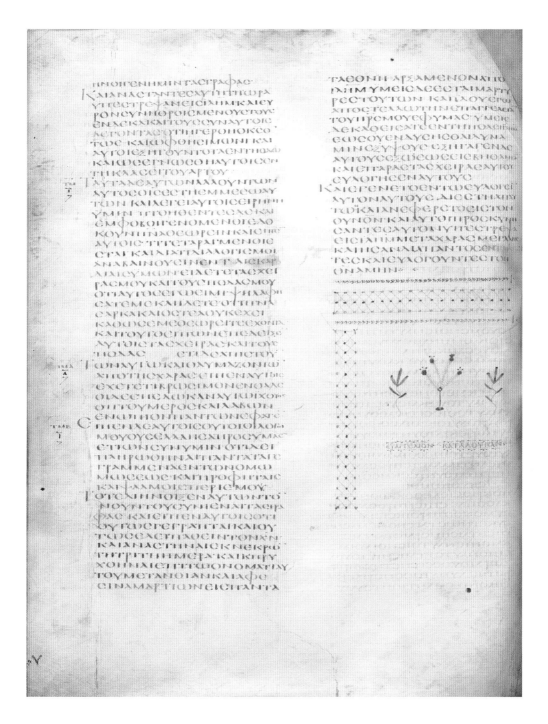

The most complete of the three earliest Christian Bibles, this copy takes its name from the capital of Greek Egypt. It is of enormous importance in establishing the biblical text, and one of the earliest books to employ significant decoration to mark major divisions of the text. The end of the Gospel of Luke is marked by a distinctive ornamental panel, or 'tailpiece' with stylized trees, perhaps an early visual reference in a manuscript to the Tree of Life.

8 End of Luke, in Greek
Codex Alexandrinus
Constantinople or Asia Minor
5th century
320 x 265 mm
Royal MS I D VIII, f. 41v

9 Abraham with angels
The Cotton Genesis
Egypt?
5th or 6th century
105 x 85 mm (shown at actual size)
Cotton MS Otho B VI, f. 26v

Although tragically damaged by fire in 1731, this manuscript in Greek still remains of central importance in the history of biblical illustration. Originally containing over 300 illustrations of the book of Genesis, it retains crucial evidence of the highly accomplished technique of late antique book painting. In this fragment Abraham greets, or possibly pleads with, the angels sent by God to destroy Sodom. Parts of the Greek text are legible above and below the image.

This luxurious leaf of very thin purple parchment once formed part of an early manuscript of the Four Gospels in Greek. Its title derives from the Latin for St Petersburg, where most of the surviving leaves are preserved. Whereas the silver ink used for most letters has blackened, gold is still visible on others. The marginal notations, which are references to parallel passages in the other Gospels, use an early numbering system, known as Ammonian sections, after the 3rd-century author Ammonius of Alexandria to whom they are attributed.

10 John 15:15–19, in Greek
Codex Purpureus Petropolitanus
Asia Minor or Syria ?
6th century
320 x 265 mm
Cotton MS Titus C XV, f. 5

11 Genesis 5:29–6:2, in Latin
The Old Latin Genesis
North Africa or Italy
5th century
170 x 55 mm (shown at actual size)
Papyrus 2052 recto

This is a great rarity. Together with only a few other manuscript fragments and some quotations embedded in early writings of Fathers of the Church, this fragment provides an important insight into the content of the Latin versions of the Old Testament that were in circulation before the 'authorized' translation of Jerome. For about half of its length it is the sole authority for an earlier 'Old Latin' version.

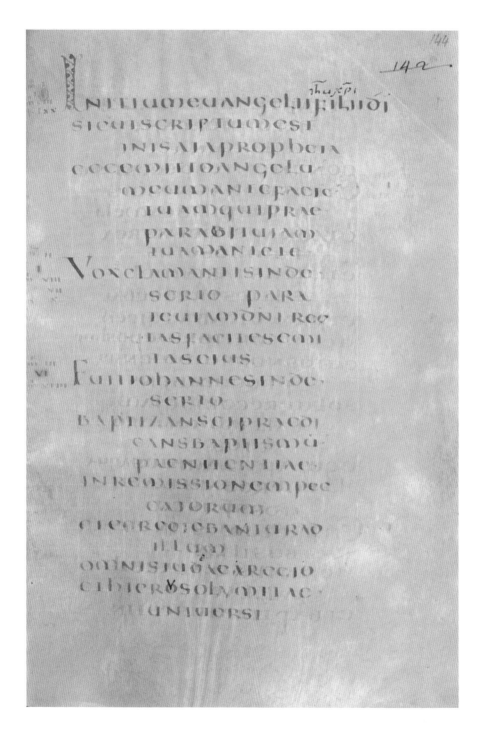

In 382 Pope Damasus commissioned the scholar Jerome to prepare a new authoritative text that could replace the various 'Old Latin' versions of the Bible. Although this manuscript retains elements of the previous translation, it forms one of the earliest surviving copies of Jerome's version, which became known as the Vulgate (from the Latin *vulgata*, meaning 'common' or 'popular'). Like many copies of the Four Gospels, this manuscript includes marginal Ammonian section numbers.

12 Mark, in Latin
Four Gospels
Northern (?) Italy
6th century
180 x 120 mm (shown at actual size)
Harley MS 1775, f. 144

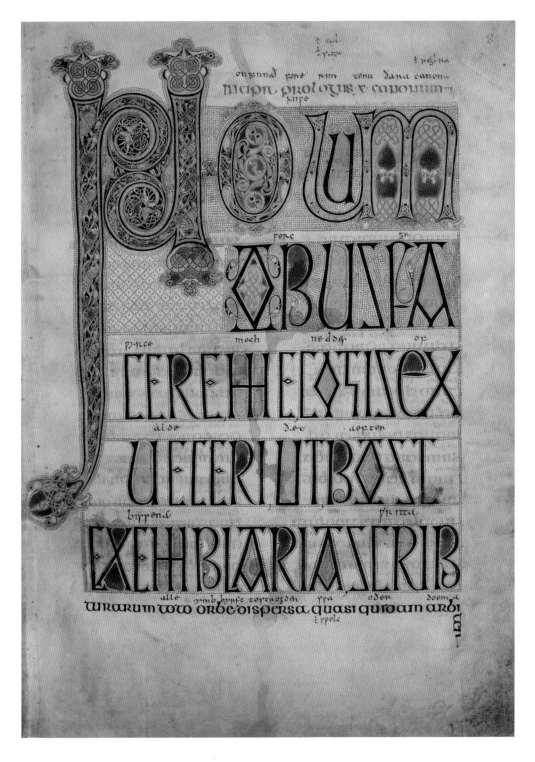

13 Jerome's letter to Pope Damasus, in Latin
The Lindisfarne Gospels
Lindisfarne, England
between 698 and 721
340 X 240 mm
Cotton MS Nero D IV, f. 3

Written and illustrated probably by Eadfrith, Bishop of Lindisfarne (698–721), the Lindisfarne Gospels is a spectacular example of the abstracted decoration characteristic of Anglo-Saxon art. Words become elements of design, as with the opening words, *Novum opus* (New work) in Jerome's letter to Pope Damasus prefacing his translation. The writing and intricate decoration of this manuscript has been interpreted as an act of personal spirituality and devotion.

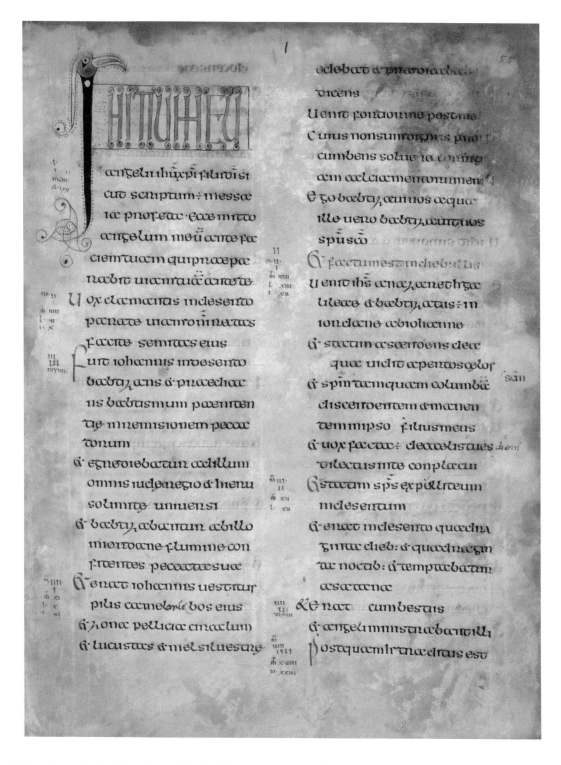

Although on a less lavish scale than the Lindisfarne Gospels, the first words of Mark's Gospel *Initium evangelii* (beginning of the Gospel) also become ornament, the first letter adorned with a bird's beak and the other initial letters decorated in a coloured panel. In contrast to the Lindisfarne Gospels (opposite), which may have been designed primarily for display, this copy appears to have been intended for regular, practical use in services.

14 Mark, in Latin
Four Gospels
Northumbria, England
8th century
285 x 215 mm
Royal MS I B VII, f. 55

The small size of this Latin copy of the Four Gospels made it easily portable; it was perhaps carried in a *cumdach* (an ornamental satchel) hung around the neck. Commonly referred to as a 'Pocket Gospel', it is one of several surviving Irish examples produced for private use, which may have been carried by priests for easy reference, or worn to protect the wearer. In a distinctively Irish interpretation of an Evangelist portrait, the frontal image of Luke includes animal interlace in the framing panels.

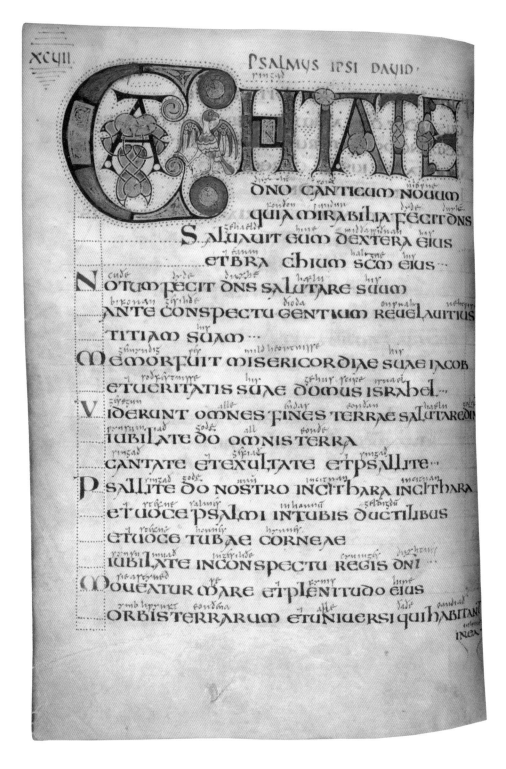

In Anglo-Saxon England, Jerome's first translation of the Psalms, the Roman version, continued to be copied, and this is the earliest surviving example of it. An Old English translation was added in the 9th century above the Latin text; this addition is the oldest extant translation into English of any biblical text. The entire first word of Psalm 98 *Cantate* (Sing), which begins the group of Psalms to be said on Saturdays, is ornamented with bright colours, with gold interlace and a small bird between the letters.

16 Psalm 98 (97) in Latin
The Vespasian Psalter
Kent, England
1st half of 8th century
235 x 180 mm
Cotton MS Vespasian A I, f. 93v

ETLOCATUSEST TIBI
CT AIT MICHEA;
CUSURUS ES INDIE ILLA QUANDO INTRE
DIERIS CUBICULUM INTRACUBICULU
UT ABSCONDARIS.
CT AIT REX ISRAHEL;
TOLLITE MICHEAM ET MANEAT APUT
AMON PRINCIPEM CIUITATIS
ET APUT IOAS FILIUM AMMELECH.
ET DICITE EIS HAEC DICIT REX;
MITTITE UIRUM ISTUM INCARCEREM
ET SUSTENTATE EUM PANE TRIBULA
TIONIS ET AQUA ANGUSTIAE.
DONEC REUERTAR INPACE;
DIXITQ MICHEAS;
SI REUERSUS FUERIS INPACE NONEST
LOCUTUS DNS INME;
ET AIT AUDITE POPULI OMNES;
ASCENDIT ITAQ REX ISRAHEL
ET IOSAPHAT REX IUDA INRAMOTH
GALAAD;
DIXITQ REX ISRAHEL ADIOSAPHAT;
SUME ARMA ET INGREDERE PROELIU.
ET INDUERE UESTIBUS TUIS;
PORRO REX ISRAHEL MUTAUIT
HABITUM ET INGRESSUS EST BELLU;
REX AUTEM SIRIAE PRAECEPERAT
PRINCIPIB CURRUUM TRIGINTA
DUOBUS DICENS
NON PUGNABITIS CONTRAMINOREM
ET MAIOREM QUEMPIAM.
NISI CONTRA REGEM ISRAHEL SOLUM;
CUM ERGO UIDISSENT PRINCIPES
CURRUUM IOSAPHAT
SUSPICATI SUNT QUOD IPSE ESSET
REX ISRAHEL.
ET IMPETU FACTO PUGNABANT
CONTRA EUM;
ET EXCLAMAUIT IOSAPHAT;
INTELLEXERUNTQ PRINCIPES
CURRUUM QUOD NON ESSET
REX ISRAHEL
ET CESSAUERUNT ABEO;
UNUS AUTEM QUIDAM TETENDIT

ARCUM ININCERTUM SAGITTAM
DIRIGENS
ET CASU PERCUSSIT REGEM ISRAHEL
INTER PULMONE ET STOMACHUM.
AT ILLE DIXIT AURIGE SUO;
UERTE MANUM TUAM ET EICE ME
DE EXERCITU
QUIA GRAUITER UULNERATUS SUM;
COMMISUM EST ERGO PROELIUM
INDIE ILLA.
ET REX ISRAHEL STABAT INCURRU SUO
CONTRA SIROS ET MORTUUS
EST UESPERI;
FLUEBAT AUTEM SANGUIS PLAGAE
INSINU CURRUS.
ET PRAECO PERSONUIT INUNIUERSO
EXERCITU ANTEQUAM SOL
OCCUMBERET DICENS
UNUSQUISQ REUERTATUR INCIUITA
TEM ET INTERRAM SUAM;
MORTUUS EST AUTEM REX
ET PERLATUS EST SAMARIAM;
SEPELIERUNTQ REGEM INSAMARIA
ET LAUERUNT CURRUM INPISCINA
SAMARIAE.
ET LINXERUNT CANES SANGUINEM EIUS
ET HABENAS LAUERUNT IUXTA
UERBUM DNI QUOD LOCUTUS FUERAT
RELIQUA UERO SERMONUM AHAB
ET UNIUERSA QUAE FECIT.
ET DOMUS EBURNEAE QUAM
AEDIFICAUIT.
CUNCTARUMQ URBIUM QUAS EX
STRUXIT
NONNE SCRIPTA SUNT HAEC INLIBRO
UERBORUM DIERUM REGUM ISRL
DORMIUIT ERGO AHAB CUM PATRIBUS SUIS
ET REGNAUIT OHOZIAS FILIUS
EIUS PRO EO;
IOSAPHAT FILIUS ASA REGNARE
COEPERAT SUPERIUDAM ANNO
QUARTO AHAB REGIS ISRAHEL.
TRIGINTA QUINQ ANNORUM ERAT
CUM REGNARE COEPISSET;

17 1 Kings (III Kings) 22:24–42, in Latin
Ceolfrid Bible leaves
Northumbria, England
between 689 and 716
480 x 340 mm
Add. MS 45025, f. 2

Scholars believe that this leaf originally formed part of one of three giant Bibles produced at the abbey of Wearmouth or Jarrow under the direction of Abbot Ceolfrid (689–716). The close relationship with Rome maintained by Ceolfrid and the high level of scholarship at the abbeys is reflected in the elegant script of this Bible. It is one of the earliest surviving manuscripts of the Old Testament written in England.

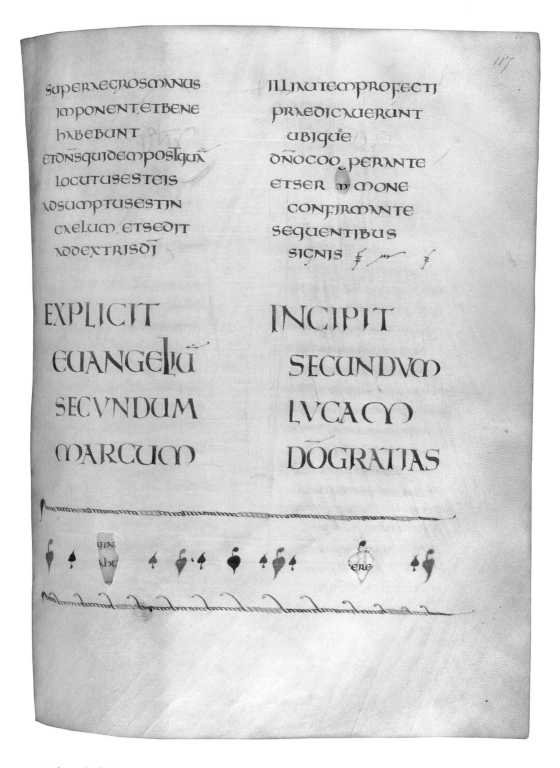

SUPERAEGROSMANUS
IMPONENT.ETBENE
HABEBUNT
ETONSQUIDEMPOSTQUA
LOCUTUSESTEIS
ADSUMPTUSESTIN
CAELUM.ETSEDIT
ADDEXTRISDI

ILLIAUTEMPROFECTI
PRAEDICAUERUNT
UBIQUE
DNOCOO PERANTE
ETSER M MONE
CONFIRMANTE
SEQUENTIBUS
SIGNIS

EXPLICIT
EUANGELIU
SECVNDUM
MARCUM

INCIPIT
SECUNDVM
LVCAM
DOGRATIAS

At the end of this manuscript the monk Lupus says that he wrote it for Abbot Ato, probably abbot of St Vincent near Benevento (739–60). In Lupus's beautiful script the words are rarely separated, being divided instead into lines that correspond to divisions of sense, as in the Bible on the facing page. The ending and beginning of each Gospel is marked by larger script and a band of restrained coloured decoration.

18 End of Mark, in Latin
Four Gospels
Benevento, Italy
middle of 8th century
350 x 275 mm
Add. MS 5463, f. 117

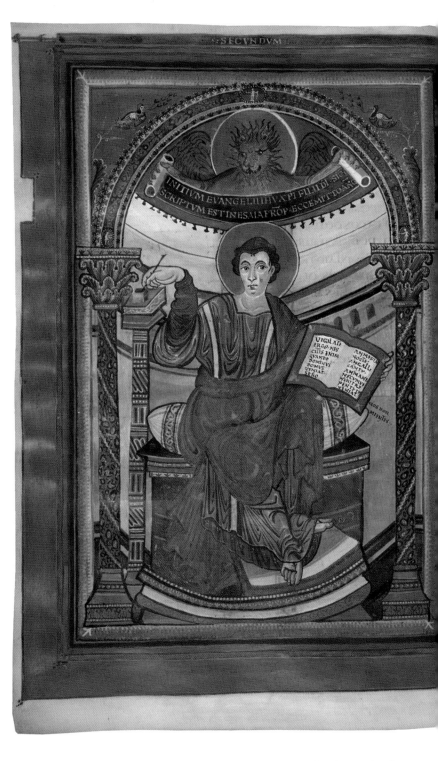

19–20 Evangelist portrait of Mark
Mark, in Latin
The Harley Golden Gospels
Aachen ?, Carolingian Empire
circa 800
365 x 250 mm
Harley MS 2788, ff. 71v–72

The group of books to which this manuscript belongs is closely associated with the Emperor Charlemagne (800–14), the first sovereign of the revived Christian Empire of the West, and with his capital at Aachen. Like its fellows, the Gospels appears to reflect the personal initiative and tastes of the emperor. Its text is written entirely in gold. As a full-page frontispiece to Mark's Gospel, the Evangelist is portrayed dipping his pen into an inkwell.

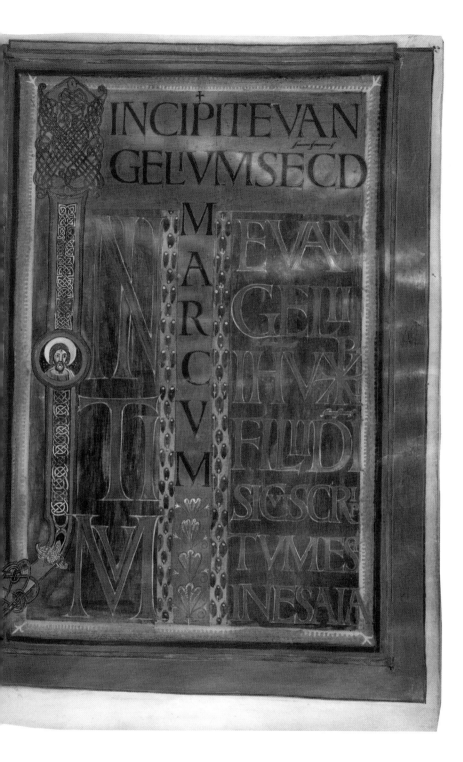

He holds a book open at the text of chapter 13:35–36, the last words of which spill over onto the background. Above him, his symbol, the lion, holds open a scroll bearing the text of the beginning of Mark. On the opposite page, the first letter of the book is decorated with interlace patterns and a roundel of Christ, while the rest of the word I(NITIUM) (beginning) is written in large gold letters. Mark's name MARCUM appears in the central column in red.

34

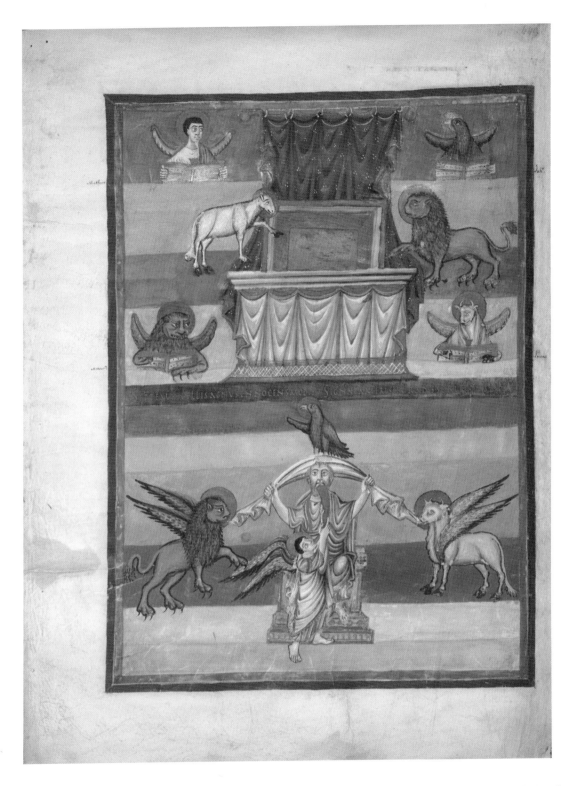

21 The Book of Seven Seals,
the Lamb, the Lion of Judah, Symbols of the
Evangelists
The Moutier-Grandval Bible
Tours, France
2nd quarter of 9th century
495 x 380 mm
Add. MS 10546, f. 449

This immense one-volume Bible of the entire Vulgate as revised by Alcuin of York (d. 804) is one of three surviving illustrated copies produced in Tours in the 9th century. This last, or explicit, page is a complex allegory of the unity of the two Testaments, drawing on imagery from Revelation, with the book 'sealed with seven seals' on an altar being opened by the Lamb and the Lion of Judah. A recent interpretation of the seated figure in the lower portion is that it is a personification of the Bible itself.

Theodulf, Bishop of Orléans (d. 821), succeeded Alcuin as an advisor to the Emperor Charlemagne, and like him, Theodulf also revised the Vulgate translation of the Bible. Only six copies of his revision survive, and this is one of the earliest. Produced under Theodulf's close supervision, it was intended to be an accessible reference work. Unlike the *Moutier-Grandval Bible* on the opposite page, it is not illustrated, but its text is nevertheless presented with distinctive clarity, conciseness, and restrained elegance.

22 Psalms 80–85 (79–84), in Latin
The St Hubert Bible
Orléans, France
1st quarter of 9th century
330 x 235 mm
Add. MS 24142, f. 124

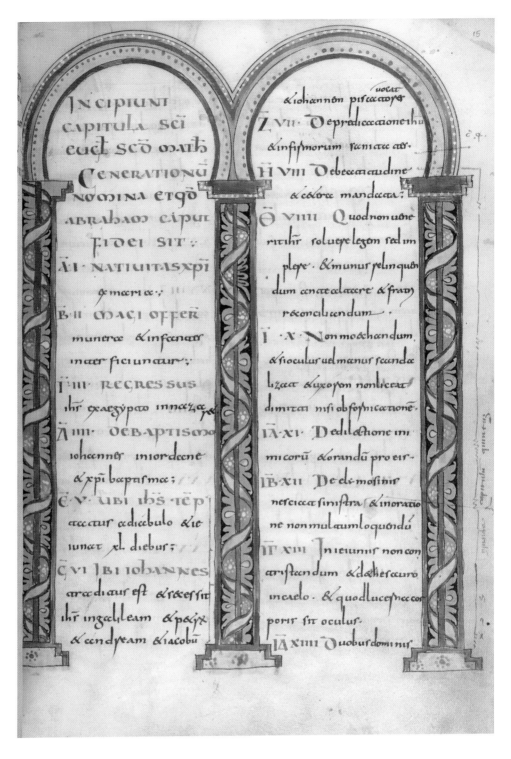

23 List of chapters, in Latin
Schuttern Gospels
Schuttern, Carolingian Empire
between c. 816 and 823
300 x 215 mm
Add. MS 47673, f. 15

Made at the Benedictine abbey of Schuttern near Strasbourg, for Abbot Bertricus (c. 816–23), this manuscript includes a table of contents in which each chapter is identified by a Greek letter and a corresponding Roman numeral in red. The numbers denote divisions of the text that preceded those of modern chapters. These divisions vary from copy to copy, depending on the version used as a model.

This image of Jerome (his name *Hieronimus* is written in gold on the background) occurs at the beginning of a luxury copy of the Psalms in Latin, named after the Emperor Lothar (840–55), Charlemagne's grandson. Enhanced with gold and silver, the portrait celebrates the author whose Latin translation of the Bible became the standard version in use in the West throughout the Middle Ages. He holds a bejewelled book, perhaps intended as a representation of an ornamented copy of his translation.

24 Portrait of Jerome
The Lothar Psalter
Aachen ?, Carolingian Empire
c. 840–55
235 x 185 mm
Add. MS 37768, f. 6

38

25 John, in Latin
Gospels of Luke and John
Corvey?, Carolingian Empire
9th century
275 x 175 mm
Egerton MS 768, f. 63

The beginning of John's Gospel is marked by a monogram of its first word, IN, decorated by the interlace and stylized animal motifs typical of Franco-Saxon ornament. Because of this decoration's blending of styles, scholars are divided on where the manuscript was made; it is now usually assigned to the Saxon abbey of Corvey in modern Westphalia, which was founded by monks from the abbey of Corbie in Picardy, northern France.

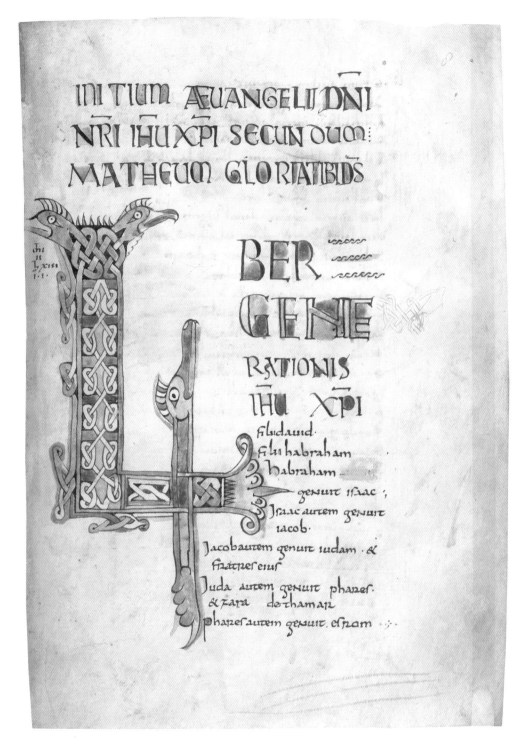

A similar method of emphasizing the initial letter of each Gospel was adopted in this manuscript. Whereas the script is in a style developed at Tours, the first word of Matthew, LI(ber) (book), is composed of interlace and bird's heads, resembling Insular ornament. Within the text the name of Jesus is often abbreviated, as here in the last line of large text IHU XPI (from the Greek Ihesu Christi).

26 Matthew, in Latin
Four Gospels
Brittany ?, western France
9th century
300 x 215 mm
Egerton MS 609, f. 8

27 Evangelist portrait of Mark
The Coronation Gospels
Lobbes, near Liège, southern Netherlands
last quarter of 9th century or 1st quarter
of 10th century
235 x 180 mm
Cotton MS Tiberius A II, f. 74v

This late Carolingian Four Gospels in Latin was acquired by King Æthelstan (d. 939), who presented it to Christ Church, Canterbury. Tradition suggests that it was later used as an oath book for coronations. The verse written in gold in the pediment associates Mark with his symbol, as a voice of a lion crying out in the wilderness. The verse is a quotation from a poem on the Bible by the 5th-century writer Sedulius. In Carolingian manuscripts the verse relating to each Evangelist often accompanies the Evangelist's portrait.

Devised by Eusebius, Bishop of Caesarea (315– c. 338/9), the Canon tables list in parallel columns the numbers of closely related sections in the Gospels. In Canon table two, shown here, the episodes common to Matthew, Mark and Luke are indicated, each identified by an abbreviated name at the top of the column: 'Mat', 'Mark' and 'Lucas'. The most common way of ornamenting Canon tables was to put them into an architectural framework with decorated columns, capitals, and classical entablature, often inhabited by animals or people.

28 Canon table, in Latin
Four Gospels
Northern France
9th century
240 x 175 mm
Harley MS 2826, f. 5

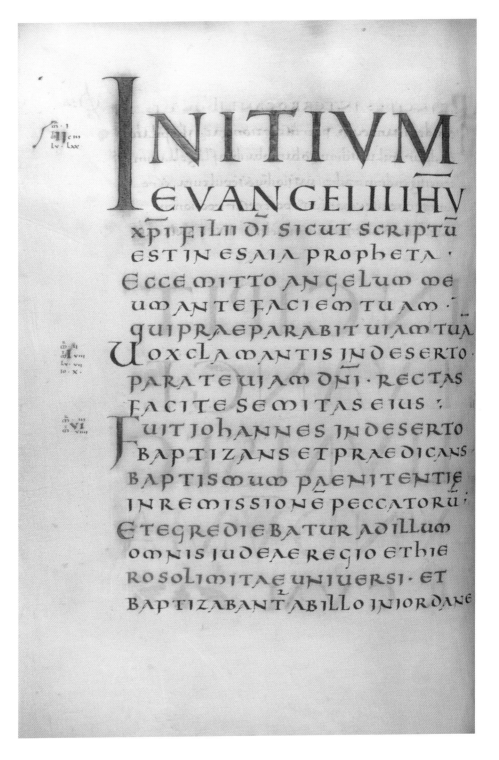

INITIVM
EVANGELII IHV
xpi filii di sicut scriptu
est in esaia propheta ·
ecce mitto angelum me
um ante faciem tuam :
qui praeparabit uiam tua
Uox clamantis in deserto ·
parate uiam dni · rectas
facite semitas eius :
Fuit johannes in deserto
baptizans et praedicans
baptismum paenitentie
in remissione peccatoru :
et egrediebatur ad illum
omnis iudeae regio et hie
rosolimitae uniuersi · et
baptizabant ab illo in iordane

29 Mark, in Latin
Four Gospels
Loire valley, France
9th century
280 x 205 mm
Harley MS 2795, f. 78v

Rich copies of Gospel books were often kept or displayed on altars, and like the liturgical vessels they accompanied, were sometimes made using precious materials. Both copies of the Four Gospels on these pages include text written in gold, the cost and value of this medium reflecting the preciousness of the scriptures they record. On this page the gold alternates with lines of red. The marginal cross-references of the Ammonian sections are also executed in gold.

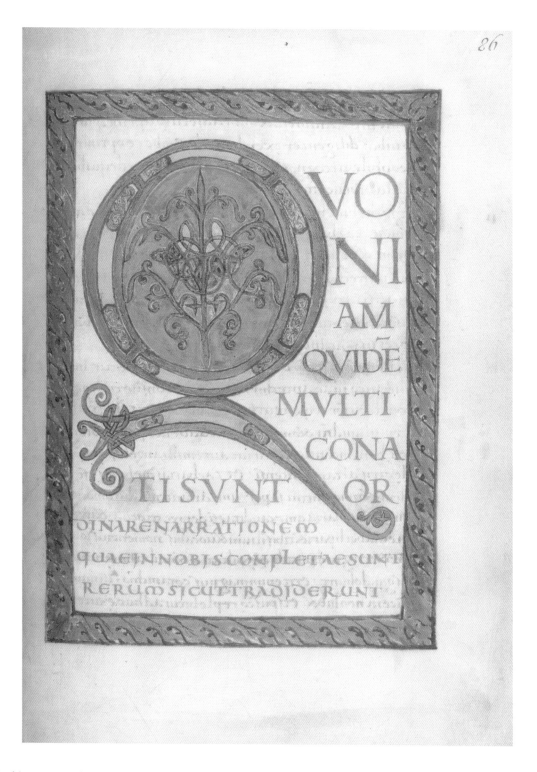

In this even more lavish copy, the entire text is written in gold. The beginning of each Gospel is also elaborate, transforming the first words into a sort of title page with added coloured decoration. The imposing first letter of Luke's Gospel, *Q(uoniam)* (Since), which takes up much of the page, demonstrates the continuing high standard of manuscript production at major centres before the development of narrative initials.

30 Luke, in Latin
Four Gospels
Northern France or Paris
3rd quarter of 9th century
265 x 190 mm
Harley MS 2797, f. 86

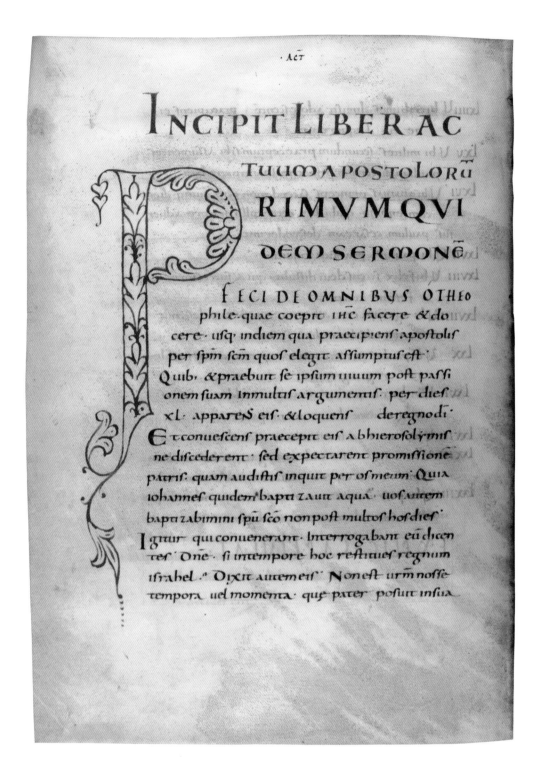

·ACT·

INCIPIT LIBER AC
TUUM APOSTOLORŪ
RIMUMQVI
DEM SERMONĒ

FECI DE OMNIBUS OTHEo
phile. quae coepit ihc facere & do
cere· usq; indiem qua praecipiens apostolis
per spm scm quos elegit assumptus est·
Quib; &praeburt se ipsum uiuum post passi
onem suam inmultis argumentis· per dies
xl· appareNs eis· &loquens deregnodi·
Et conuescens praecepit eis abhierosolymis
ne discederent· sed expectarent promissionē
patris· quam audistis inquit per osmeum Quia
iohannes quidem bapti zauit aqua· uos autem
bapti zabimini spū sco non post multos hos dies·
Igitur qui conuenerant· interrogabant eū dicen
tes· Dne· si intempore hoc restitues regnum
isrnhel· Dixit autem eis· Non est urm nosse
tempora uel momenta· quę pater posuit insua

31 Acts, in Latin
Acts, Epistles, Revelation
St Gall, Switzerland
between 872 and 883
235 x 165 mm
Add. MS 11852, f. 122v

These pages exhibit further examples of volumes containing only a selection of biblical texts, rather than the complete canon now standard in Christian Bibles. This manuscript contains the New Testament except for the Four Gospels, as well as the apocryphal Epistle of Paul to the Laodiceans. It was produced at the important monastic centre of St Gall under Abbot Hartmut (872–83), and is written in elegant script, with restrained decoration of red penwork initials.

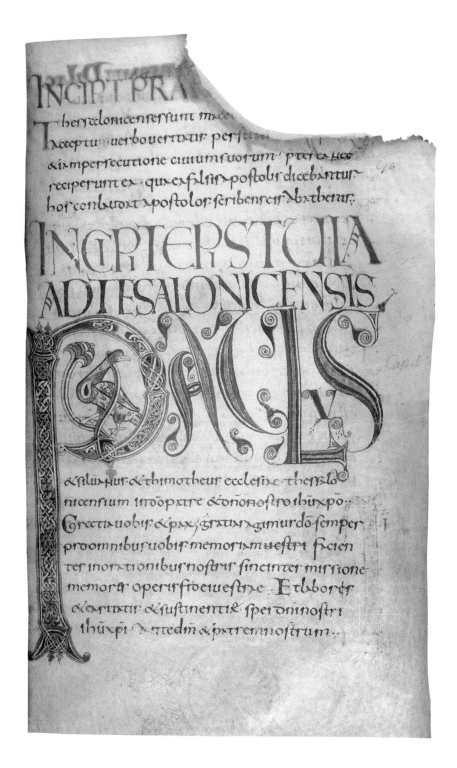

This manuscript includes what are known as the Pauline Epistles (the letters written by the Apostle Paul), most of the Catholic Epistles (other New Testament letters, which were not addressed to any particular person but rather to the universal church), and Revelation. It was probably made in Rheims under Archbishop Hincmar (845–82). At the beginning of Paul's letter to the Thessalonians his name (*Paulus*) is decorated with elements of interlace and a stylized bird within the ornamental letter P.

32 1 Thessalonians, in Latin
Epistles, Revelation
Rheims, France
2nd half of 9th century
290 x 185 mm
Harley MS 1772, f. 75

33 Christ in Majesty with All Saints
The Æthelstan Psalter
Winchester ?, England
2nd quarter of 10th century (image)
130 x 90 mm (shown at actual size)
Cotton MS Galba A XVIII, f. 21

According to tradition, this Psalter in Latin of Continental origin was owned by King Æthelstan (d. 939) and given by him to Winchester Cathedral. One of the four full-page images added to it in England depicts Christ in Majesty surrounded by 'the chorus of martyrs, confessors, and virgins'. Christ displays his wounds, and is labelled as the *A(lpha)* and *ω(Omega)*, the beginning and end. In the crowded compartments tonsured monks and women with covered heads are visible.

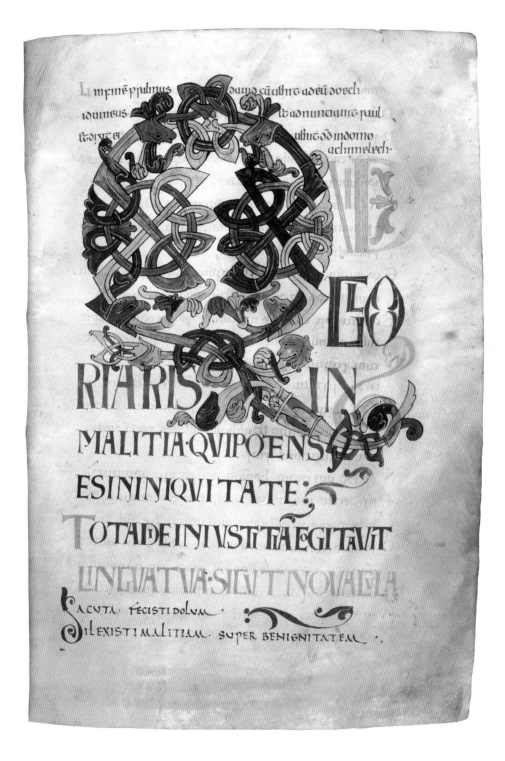

This Psalter is of great importance for the purity of its text of Jerome's Roman version of the Psalms. The liturgical divisions are marked by large multi-coloured display script. This one, at the beginning of Psalm 52 (in current numbering) is a division found in English, but not most Continental manuscripts. The first letter of *Quid gloriaris* (Why do you boast?) is decorated with woven tendrils and animal heads.

34 Psalm 52 (51), in Latin
The Bosworth Psalter
Canterbury ?, England
last quarter of 10th century
390 x 265 mm
Add. MS 37517, f. 33

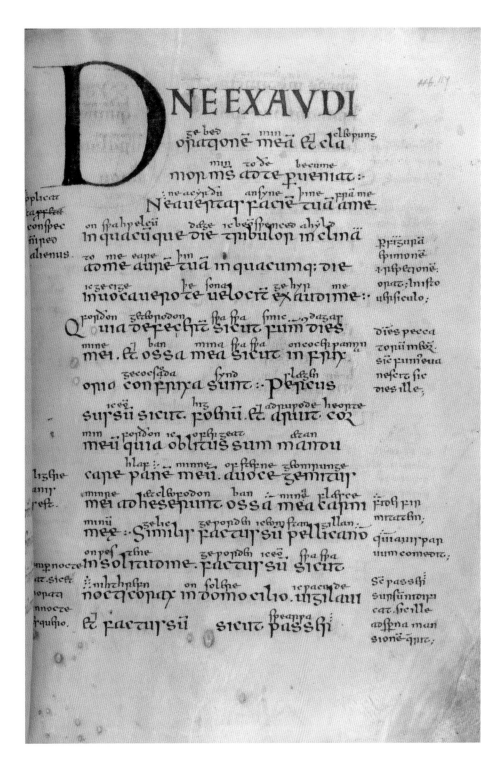

35 Psalm 102 (101), in Latin with Old English
Psalter
Winchester, England
10th century
265 x 185 mm
Royal MS 2 B V, f. 117

This Anglo-Saxon copy of the Psalms is of Jerome's Roman version, rather
than the Gallican translation found in most Continental manuscripts.
English copies also tend to divide the Psalms into three groups of 50 Psalms,
enlarging or decorating the initial at the beginning of Psalms 1, 51 and 101,
as seen here in the initial word D[omi]ne. In this copy the scribe added an Old
English translation, in smaller script, between the lines, confirming
the manuscript's English origin.

The *Heliand* is a 9th-century poem in which the Four Gospels have been transformed into Old Saxon alliterative verse. Like the *Diatesseron*, on which it is apparently based, the poem combines the Four Gospels into a single narrative account. It derives its name from the appellation *Heliand*, or Saviour, given to Jesus, who is characterized in the poem as the 'mighty Chieftain' or 'Ruler', and the Apostles as his 'warrior companions' or 'thanes'. This manuscript is one of only two complete copies of the text to survive.

36 Heliand, in Old Saxon with some Latin
Heliand
Southern England
2nd half of 10th century
220 x 140 mm
Cotton MS Caligula A VII, f. 132

37 John 11:47–56, in Old English
Four Gospels
Southern England
1st half of 11th century
245 x 150 mm
Cotton MS Otho C I, part I, f. 94

This 11th-century copy of the Four Gospels in English demonstrates that English biblical translations existed long before the Reformation. Although damaged by fire in 1731, this volume remains an important witness of an Old English translation. At the end of John's Gospel the scribe recorded his name: 'Wulfwi me wrat.' Wulfwi may also have been responsible for the simple decorated initials.

An organized system of shorthand for Latin that was developed in the 1st century BC for recording speeches in the Senate is attributed to Marcus Tullius Tiro (103–4 BC), a slave and later freedman of the Roman statesman Cicero. Unusually, this system of abbreviations is employed in this small Psalter. Only the headings or divisions of Psalms are given in Latin, written in red.

38 Psalm 119:55–76 (118:55–76), in Tironian shorthand with Latin Psalter
Rheims, France
10th century
155 x 115 mm
Add. MS 9046, ff. 74v-75

52

39–40 Portrait of Luke
Acts, in Greek
New Testament
Constantinople
middle of 10th century
290 x 210 mm
Add. MS 28815, ff. 162v–163

Arguably the most beautiful Byzantine manuscript of the New Testament possessed by the British Library marks the opening of Acts with a fine standing portrait of its supposed author, Luke. The manuscript also includes two seated portraits of Luke and John at the beginning of their Gospels, a decorated headpiece at the start of each book, with traces of purple leaves, and Greek text written in gold. Together, these features bear vivid witness to the extremely high standard of production of books in Greek that prevailed at

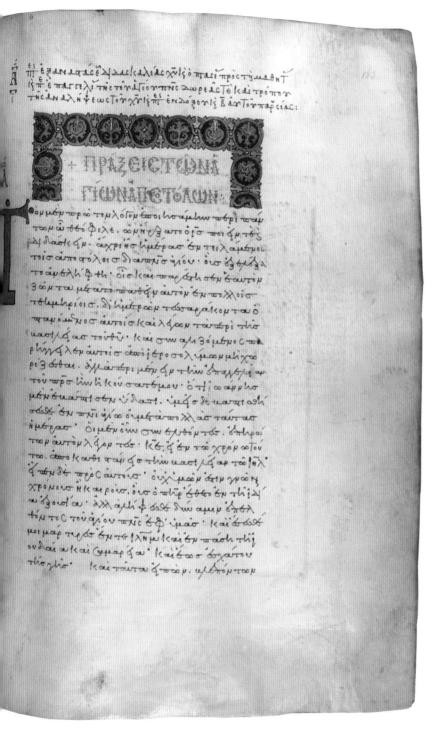

the capital of eastern Christendom following the defeat in 843 of Iconoclasm, the religious movement that denied the holiness of icons and rejected their veneration. The portrait of Luke reflects both the Christian and classical inheritances of Constantinople, blending Christian unworldliness and classical physicality. The front cover of the book is also richly decorated, suggesting that it may have been used processionally in the liturgy, at least in later times.

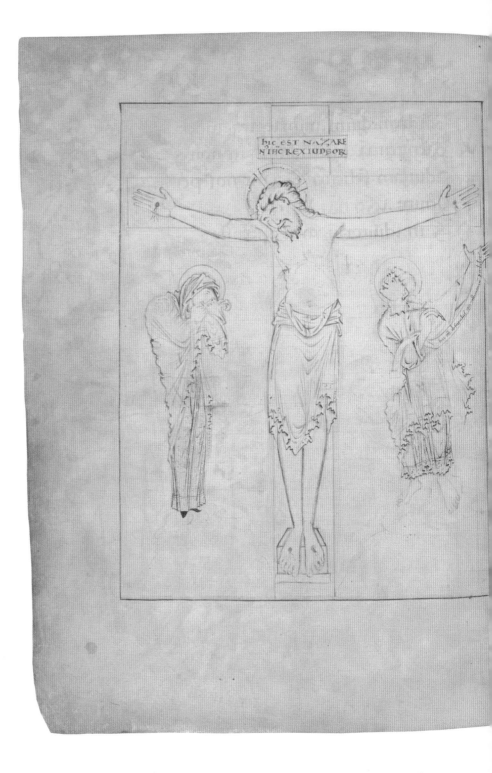

This imposing copy of the Psalms in Jerome's Gallican version may have been intended for the personal use of Oswald (d. 992), Bishop of Worcester and Archbishop of York, who profoundly influenced the development of the English church during the second half of the 10th century. It certainly contains liturgical evidence linking it with one of Oswald's foundations, the Benedictine monastery of Ramsey in Huntingdonshire. The tinted outline drawing style of

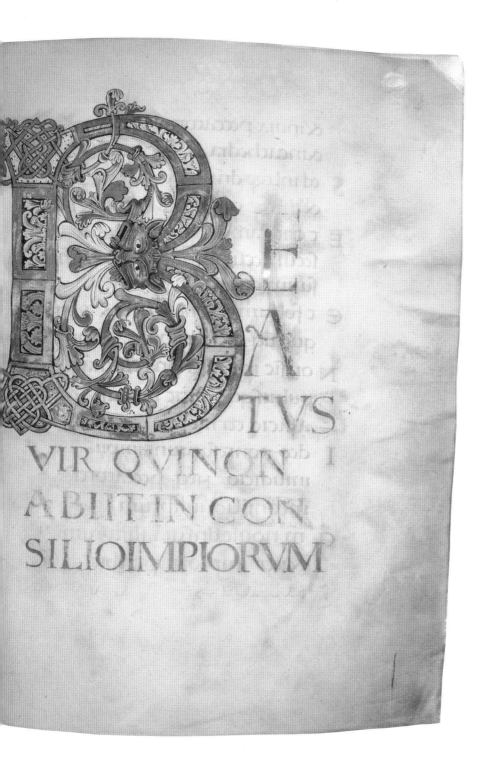

BEATVS
VIR QVINON
ABIIT IN CON
SILIOIMPIORVM

the prefatory Crucifixion is characteristic of Anglo-Saxon England and contrasts with the bright gold of the text on the opposite page. The small text scroll held by John reads 'This is the disciple who testifies to these things' (John 21:24). The decoration of the initial 'B' of the first word of the Psalms, *Beatus* (Blessed), later became standard in English Psalters, and here is a fine example of the 'Winchester School' style of illumination.

43 Canon table, in Latin
The Bury Gospels
Bury St Edmunds or Canterbury, England
1st half of 11th century
265 x 200 mm
Harley MS 76, f. 8v

In its original state, this must have been one of the most lavishly decorated books produced in 11th-century England. Its Canon tables presenting parallel Gospel passages are particularly richly ornamented. This second Canon, listing passages occurring in each of Mathew, Mark and Luke, is surmounted by a depiction of Christ, who is shown holding a book and blessing, flanked by angels. The Gospels might have been a gift to the monastery of Bury St Edmunds, founded by King Cnut in 1020.

This richly decorated manuscript of the Four Gospels takes its name from a copy of a letter included at the end of the volume regarding a monk called Grimbald (d. 901). As in many medieval copies, the beginning of each Gospel in this richly decorated manuscript takes up an entire page. Here the first words of John's text are framed by groups of figures looking up to a central medallion of the *Virgin and Child*, perhaps alluding to the Incarnation discussed in the first chapter.

44 Blessed adoring the Virgin Mary and Christ
John, in Latin
The Grimbald Gospels
Canterbury or Winchester, England
1st quarter of 11th century
325 x 245 mm
Add. MS 34890, f. 115

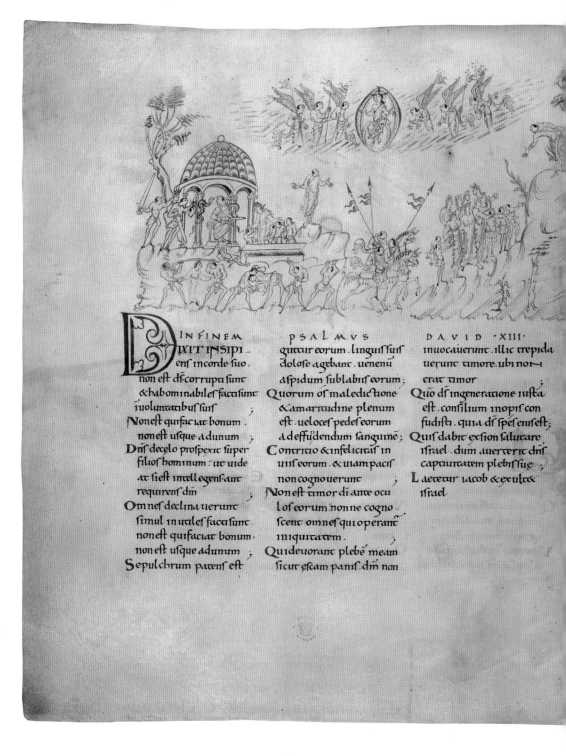

IN FINEM
DIXIT INSIPI_
ens incorde suo.
non est dscorrupti sunt
&habominabiles facti sunt
iuoluntatibus suis   ;
Non est qui faciat bonum .
non est usque ad unum   ;
Dns de celo prospexit super
filios hominum : ut uide
at si est intellegens aut
requirens dm   ;
Omnes declinauerunt
simul inutiles facti sunt .
non est qui faciat bonum ·
non est usque ad unum   ;
Sepulchrum patens est

PSALMVS

gutturr eorum . linguis suis
dolose agebant . uenenu
aspidum sublabus eorum;
Quorum os maledictione
& amaritudine plenum
est . ueloces pedes eorum
ad effundendum sanguine;
Contritio & infelicitas in
uiis eorum . & uiam pacis
non cognouerunt   ;
Non est timor di ante ocu
los eorum . nonne cogno _
scent omnes qui operant
iniquitatem .
Qui deuorant plebe meam
sicut escam panis . dm non

DAVID ·XIII·

inuocauerunt . illic trepida
uerunt timore . ubi non_
erat timor
Quo ds in generatione iusta
est . consilium inopis con
fudisti . quia ds spes eius est;
Quis dabit ex sion salutare
israel . dum auertertt dns
captiuitatem plebis sue   ;
Laetetur iacob & exultet
israel

45–46 Psalms 14–15 (13–14), in Latin
The Harley Psalter
Canterbury, England
1st half of 11th century
380 x 310 mm
Harley MS 603, ff. 7v-8

This manuscript, one of the greatest masterpieces of late Anglo-Saxon book decoration, is the earliest of three surviving copies of a remarkable Carolingian manuscript, the *Utrecht Psalter*, which was apparently brought to Canterbury in the late 10th century. Its line drawings are much livelier and convey a greater sense of movement than those of the Carolingian original. In other respects most of the illustrations are remarkably true to their model, which illustrates the Psalms by translating them virtually

8

PSALMVS   DAVID   ·XIIII·

Ne quis habita
bit intabernaculo
tuo. aut quis requiesc& in
monte scō tuo

Quingreditur sine macula.
& opera tur iustitiam

Quiloquitur uertitatem in
corde suo. & nonegit dolu
inlingua sua

Nec fecit proximo suo malu.
& obprobrium non accepit

aduersus proximum suu;
Adnihilum deductus est
inconspectu eius maligñ.
timentes autem dñm
magnificat

Quiiurat proximo suo &
non decipit eu. qui pec
cuniam suam nondedit
adusuram. & munera
super innocentem non
accepit

Quifacit hęc. noncommo
uebitur ineternum

phrase-by-phrase into visual form. At the top of the left-hand page, seated in
the sky surrounded by angels, 'the Lord looks down from heaven', to find that
men are 'evildoers', shown fighting (Psalm 14:2–4). The central crowd looking
up towards the hill perhaps represents those 'expecting salvation' (Psalm 14:7).
The Psalmist then asks 'who may dwell in your sanctuary?', and on the facing
page, Psalm 15 is illustrated by those 'whose walk is blameless' including, in
the centre, a man who 'lends money to the poor without interest'.

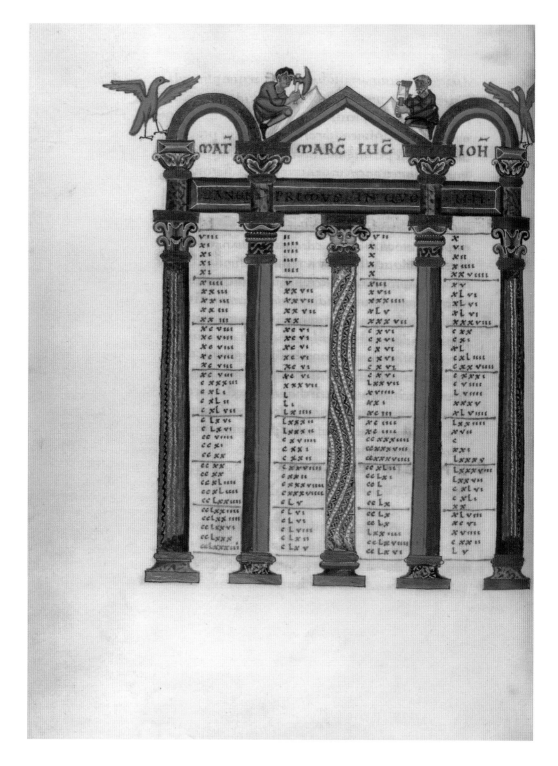

47 Canon table, in Latin
Four Gospels
Echternach, near Trier, Germany
middle of 11th century
255 x 190 mm
Harley MS 2821, f. 8v

Like the Four Gospels reproduced overleaf (*figs.* 49–50), this luxury manuscript demonstrates the high standard of production at the abbey of St Willibrord in Echternach. Its Canon tables are enclosed within highly finished architectural frames with columns separating the lists for each Gospel. The columns are most numerous in this Canon one, which compares passages appearing in each of the Four Gospels. Above, masons work on the construction of the central pediment.

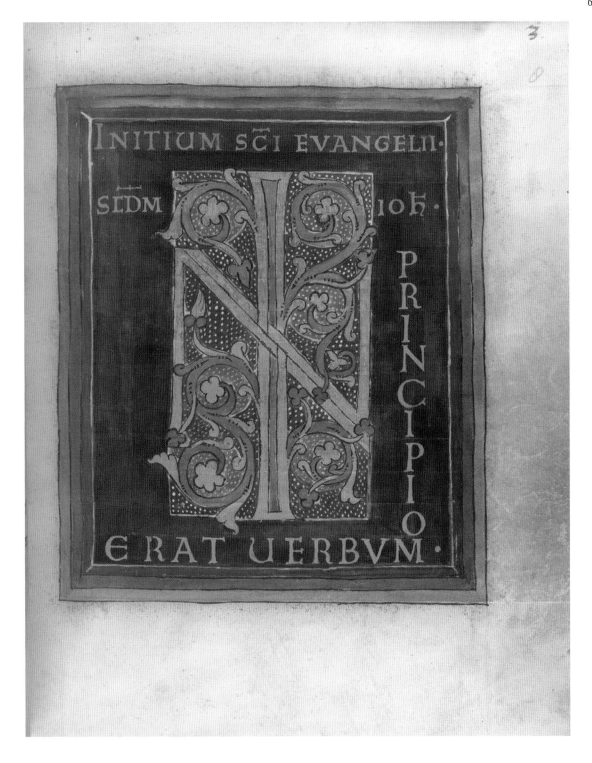

In this opulent Lectionary, with initials and illustrations executed in silver and gold, such as the monogram here of IN, the first word of John, each Gospel text is arranged according to its use in services throughout the liturgical year. The Lectionary takes its name from a prominent inscription at the beginning of the manuscript written in gold: 'God, be merciful to Odalricus, a sinner.' Odalricus may be the manuscript's scribe or artist, or perhaps its patron.

48 John, in Latin
The Odalricus Peccator Gospel Lectionary
Lorsch ?, near Worms, Germany
1st quarter of 11th century
205 x 165 mm
Harley MS 2970, f. 8

49–50 Evangelist portrait of Mark, and Nativity
Four Gospels
Echternach, near Trier, Germany
middle or 3rd quarter of 11th century
235 x 170 mm
Egerton MS 608, ff. 59v-60

Although there are no clues to suggest for whom this copy of the Four Gospels in Latin was originally produced, it was apparently designed for ceremonial use. Its original binding of oak boards, which are now studded with nail holes, was once covered with gold or silver. A hollow in the front cover probably once contained an ivory or metalwork plaque, and perhaps relics. Gold also features in the book's Evangelist portraits and the elaborate

decoration of the first letter or word of each Gospel. In addition, a full-page image of an important event in the life of Christ faces each Evangelist portrait; here Mark is seated opposite the Nativity. All these features are typical of the artistic production of the abbey of St Willibrord, Echternach, in modern-day Luxembourg, from which the Holy Roman Emperor Henry III (1039–56) is known to have ordered manuscripts.

51 Adam naming the animals
Genesis, in Old English
The Old English Hexateuch
Canterbury, England
1st half of 11th century
330 × 220 mm
Cotton MS Claudius B IV, f. 4

As the earliest copy in English of part of the Old Testament, and with over 400 illustrations, this manuscript is both remarkable and unique. Its Old English versions of Genesis, Exodus, Leviticus, Numbers, Deuteronomy and Joshua are partly the work of the Benedictine monk Aelfric (d. 1020). His scholarly paraphrases aimed to offer non-clerical readers insight into the sacred text of the Vulgate. The dominance of the vivid illustrations may indicate that this copy was commissioned for such a lay person.

INCIPIT·
EVAN
GELI
VM·SECVN
DVM MA
THEV̄· IBER

GENERATIONIS·
ihūxp̄i filii dauid· filii
abraham· Abraham
genuit ẏ saac· ẏ saac autē
genuit iacob· Iacob autē
genuit iudam· et fratres ei̅
iudas autem genuit phares·
et ʒara dethamar· fares
autē genuit esrom· Esrom
autē genuit aram· Aram

A colour wash was used to highlight words and decoration in this Italian Lectionary of Gospel readings. To accompany Matthew's genealogy of Christ at the beginning of his Gospel the artist decorated the first letter. In addition, the artist depicted Matthew writing, Matthew's symbol of a winged man, and the Annunciation of the angel Gabriel to Mary announcing that she had been chosen to bear the Christ Child.

52 Evangelist portrait of Matthew, Annunciation
Matthew, in Latin
Gospel Lectionary
Rome
last quarter of 11th century
335 x 250 mm
Add. MS 6156, f. 24

53–54 Holy Women at the Tomb,
Harrowing of Hell
The Tiberius Psalter
Winchester, England
middle or 3rd quarter of 11th century
245 x 150 mm
Cotton MS Tiberius C VI, ff. 13v-14

This Psalter is justly famous for its 24 vibrant drawings in coloured outline depicting episodes from the lives of both Christ and King David. (According to a long tradition, David was considered to have been the author of the Psalms.) The idea of preceding the text of the Psalms with such images seems to have originated in England, and this is the earliest surviving example. Such use of prefatory cycles later became extremely popular both in England and on

the Continent. The drawings in this manuscript are extraordinarily expressive and vivid. Here, on the left, the three women discover the open tomb and a huge angel. To the right, Christ, trampling a devil with bound arms and feet, breaks open the door of Hell and bends down deeply to harrow (or harass) Hell by rescuing souls from Hell's mouth.

55 Solomon praying, David and Gideon foretelling the Annunciation
Psalm 72 (71), in Greek
The Theodore Psalter
Constantinople
1066
230 x 200 mm
Add. MS 19352, f. 91v

Written and decorated by one person, this manuscript is one of the most profusely illustrated Psalters. Made for Michael, Abbot of the Studios monastery in Constantinople, it is named after its scribe and illuminator the monk, Theodore, who came to Studios from Caesarea in Cappadocia. Its 435 marginal illustrations act as a visual Christian commentary on the text of the Psalms, including David and Gideon pointing to an icon of the Virgin (left), beside the Annunciation (right).

Most illuminated Greek biblical manuscripts mark the beginning of each book with a headpiece, or decorative band, often, as here, incorporating gold and painted flowers. In contrast to the Psalter opposite, the outer margins include a textual, not pictorial, commentary, carefully arranged around the central text, at the beginning of the Catholic Epistles. Two separate passages of commentary in the right-hand and lower margins, marked A and B, are keyed into the text using the same two letters.

56 James, in Greek
Greek New Testament
Eastern Mediterranean
11th century
245 x 200 mm
Add. MS 19392A, f. 2

70

57 David harping
The Mar Saba Psalter
Jerusalem
c. 1090
120 x 95 mm (shown at actual size)
Add. MS 36928, f. 44v

The two tiny copies of the Psalms reproduced here and on the facing page were designed to be held in the hand. They offer an intimate connection with this central text. Because the Psalms are religious songs or chants, David is often shown playing the harp, or with musicians, before the beginning of the book. In this copy made at the Greek monastery of Mar Saba (St Saba in Aramaic) in Jerusalem, David is accompanied by a female figure, perhaps a personification of Melodia, borrowed from classical imagery.

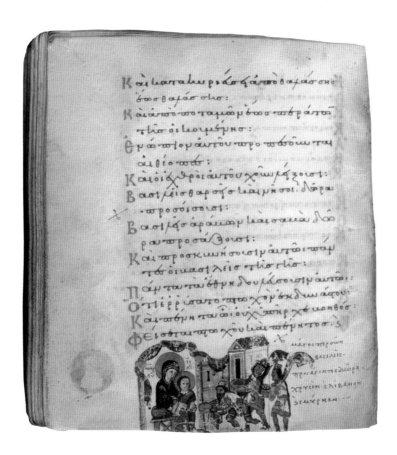

Like the *Theodore Psalter* (fig. 55), this manuscript is one of the few so-called marginal Psalters to survive, with numerous small images painted in the broad margins. Its 104 subjects illustrate and interpret the text of the Psalms, partly by foreshadowing events of the New Testament. On this page the image of the Magi bringing gifts to the Christ Child offers a Christian interpretation of the verse (Psalm 72:10): 'The kings of Tarshish and of distant shores will bring tribute to him; the kings of Sheba and Seba will present him gifts.'

58 Adoration of the Magi
Psalm 72 (71) in Greek
The Bristol Psalter
Constantinople
1st half of 11th century
105 x 90 mm (shown at actual size)
Add. MS 40731, f. 115v

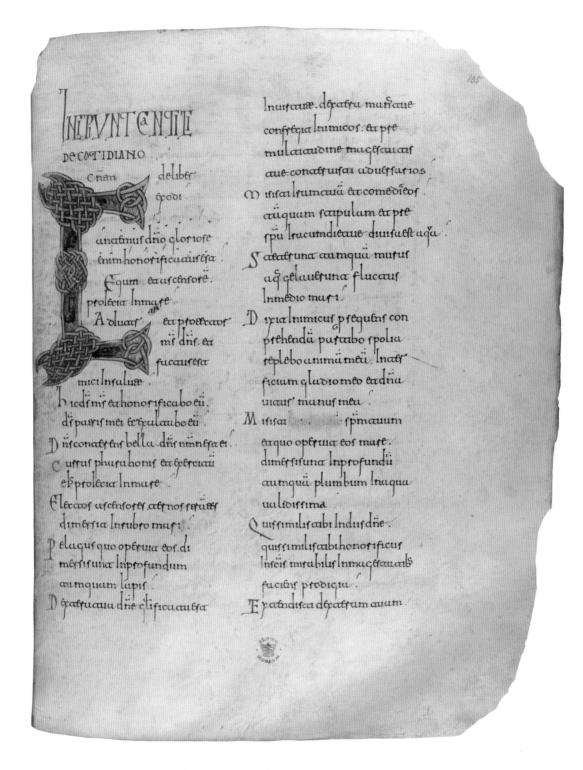

59 Canticles, in Latin
Mozarabic Psalter
Silos, Spain
11th century
390 × 300 mm
Add. MS 30851, f. 105

Songs drawn from different biblical books are placed together to form the Canticles, and often follow the Psalms in medieval manuscripts. Appropriately, the first lines beginning with *Cantemus Domino* (Let us sing to the Lord) are noted for singing. This Canticle of Moses, taken from Exodus 15, is decorated with an interlace initial. Both this manuscript and the *Silos Apocalypse* on the opposite page were made in the scriptorium of the abbey of San Sebastián in Silos, near Burgos, in northern Spain.

This manuscript is one of more than 20 copies of a commentary on the book of Revelation that was illustrated in medieval Spain. Amongst the 82 images accompanying its Latin text is this bold and dramatic representation of John's vision of Christ in Majesty. Christ is accompanied by the 24 elders of the Apocalypse, depicted in bands of vivid colour, with golden disks above their heads, inscribed with the letters *CORONAS AUREAS* (partially visible in the detail on pp 4–5). Flanking Christ are seven lamps, illustrating Revelation 4:5.

60 John's vision of Christ in Majesty
The Silos Apocalypse
Silos, Spain
1091 (text) and 1109 (decoration)
380 x 240 mm
Add. MS 11695, f. 83

61 Evangelist portrait of Mark
Cologne Gospels
Cologne, Germany
last quarter of 11th century
280 x 205 mm
Harley MS 2820, f. 78

Continuing the tradition of lavishly decorated Rhenish Gospel books in Latin, this manuscript includes rich architectural Canon tables and purple parchment with gold writing. It also contains four full-page portraits in a distinctive style, each depicting the Evangelist in the act of writing his Gospel. In the open book, below ink pots and various writing tools, the words of Mark's text in stylized form are just visible.

Decorated pages also precede each of the Four Gospels written in Latin in this French manuscript. While some are painted in bright colours, others remain unfinished as line drawings only, which now allow their draftmanship to be admired. The borders of this illustrated page are populated by figures of angels and of the blessed. As in the portrait of Mark on the opposite page, the Evangelist holds a quill. Here he also holds a knife to sharpen his quill, and an angel is present to provide inspiration.

62 Evangelist portrait of Mark, Angels, the Blessed, Christ in Majesty
Jumièges Gospels
Jumièges ?, Normandy, France
c. 1100
300 x 230 mm
Add. MS 17739, f. 69

63 Job blessing his sons and daughters
Job, in Latin
The Stavelot Bible
Stavelot, near Liège, southern Netherlands
1093–97
580 x 390 mm
Add. MS 28107, f. 4v

The writing, decoration and binding of this immense Bible made for the abbey of Stavelot took four years to complete. Two monks involved in its production, Godderan and Ernesto, are identified in an inscription, although their roles are not specified: Godderan may have been the sole scribe, and Ernesto one of the artists. At the beginning of the book of Job the artist depicted an enthroned Job blessing his seven sons and three daughters, as mentioned in the first verse below the image.

This flamboyant copy of the Four Gospels was decorated at the Benedictine abbey of Préaux near Rouen. Executed in bright colours, men, animals, and hybrid creatures climb or sit on the frame of the elaborate first letter L(iber) (Book) of Matthew's Gospel. As in earlier copies, the 'sacred name' of Christ is abbreviated as XPI (the last word on this page) and the Ammonian section references are included in the margin.

64 Matthew, in Latin
Préaux Gospels
St Pierre de Préaux, Normandy, France
last quarter of 11th century
275 x 185 mm
Add. MS 11850, f. 18

Sinicium scī evangelii secdm iohem.
In principio erat verbum. Et ver
bum erat apud deum. Et deus erat
uerbum. Hoc erat inprincipio apud
deum. Omnia p ipsum facta sunt/ &
sine ipso factum est michil. Quod fac
tum est/ inipso uita erat. Et uita erat
lux hominum! & lux intenebris lu
cet. & tenebre eam non conpreben
derunt. Fuit homo missus adeo! cui
nomen erat iohannes. Hic uenit in
testimonium. ut testimonium per

65 Evangelist portrait of John
John, in Latin
Four Gospels
Erfurt, Germany
1st quarter of 12th century
330 x 190 mm
Add. MS 14813, f. 90v

Many different combinations of decoration and text are possible, and artists regularly explored varied solutions in individualised luxury copies of medieval manuscripts. Here John's Evangelist portrait is combined with the text page, and is set against a burnished gold ground, protected by a silk curtain. (The yellow silk of the curtain for this Gospel is partially visible on the left of the image.) John prepares his quill pen with a knife above the first letter of his Gospel I(n), which is written in silver and gold.

Instead of depictions of each of the Evangelists, this elegant Latin Lectionary contains four full-page images of important events celebrated throughout the Christian year: Christmas, Easter, Ascension Day and Pentecost. Prefacing a reading from Mark 16:14–18 for Ascension Day, Christ ascends to heaven, in a partial mandorla typically used for Christ or God, (named after the Italian for almond), while the Apostles and Mary stand below.

66 Ascension
Gospel Lectionary
Hirsau ?, southern Germany
c. 1100
260 x 185 mm
Egerton MS 809, f. 33v

67 Elimelech, Naomi, and their sons
Ruth, in Latin
Montpellier Bible
Southern France
1st quarter of 12th century
510 x 370 mm
Harley MS 4772, f. 120v (detail)

A large and ambitious project, this two-volume Bible is decorated with initials containing geometric interlace and representations of biblical figures. The book of Ruth opens with an image of Elimelech, Naomi and their sons on their journey to Moab, the first known occurrence of this depiction in medieval art. The initial is decorated also by two sirens or hybrids, which have a less clear connection with the text.

Intricate and dense interlace, featuring white beasts and bright animal heads
is a characteristic feature of manuscripts associated with Monte Cassino,
where Benedict developed his monastic Rule. Appropriately, the large initials
in this Psalter mark the Benedictine division of the Psalms, rather than the
more common Roman divisions. The Psalter's distinctive Beneventan script
was developed in southern Italy, and includes many distinctive letter forms,
such as the tall looped 'e' in the first word of the last line (medio).

68 Psalm 74 (73), in Latin
Monte Cassino Psalter
Southern Italy
middle of 12th century
200 x 130 mm
Add. MS 18859, f. 39

69 Elkanah and his wives
1 Samuel (1 Kings), in Latin
The Rochester Bible
Rochester, England
1st half of 12th century
395 x 265 mm
Royal MS I C VII, f. 58 (detail)

The earliest English Romanesque examples of initial letters containing narrative scenes related to the text occur in this Bible from the cathedral priory of St Andrew, Rochester. The text of 1 Samuel is illustrated with Elkanah and his two wives, one holding children on her lap. This is a succinct summary of the first verses, which include the statement: 'He [Elkanah] had two wives; one was called Hannah and the other Peninnah. Peninnah had children, but Hannah had none.'

This elaborate Latin Psalter may have been commissioned by Henry of Blois, Bishop of Winchester (1129–71), and younger brother of King Stephen. It illustrates the continuing production of the Psalms as a separate book, often as a luxury copy. Thirty-eight pages of narrative illustrations of subjects from both Testaments preface the Psalms, executed with colour washes. As part of a sequence of scenes from the life of Christ, Mary and Joseph flank the young Jesus, above his Baptism.

70 Christ between his parents, Baptism
The Winchester Psalter
Winchester, England
middle of 12th century
320 x 200 mm
Cotton MS Nero C IV, f. 16

71 Psalm 39 (38), in Latin
The Melisende Psalter
Crusader kingdom of Jerusalem
between 1131 and 1143
215 x 140 mm
Egerton MS 1139, f. 60v

The probable first owner of this Psalter was Melisende, Queen of Jerusalem, when the Holy Land was ruled by the Crusaders. The manuscript mirrors the hybrid cultural milieu of its owner, with its Latin text preceded by 24 images of the life of Christ painted in a Byzantine style on gold backgrounds. Large initials at the divisions of the Psalms were also executed in gold, this one with a man and a dog enmeshed in foliage. Such decoration has no apparent direct connection to the text.

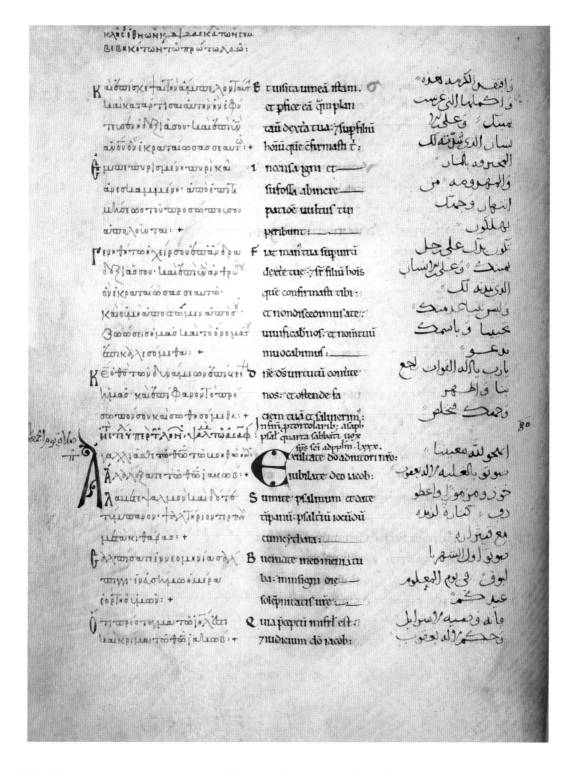

When the present manuscript was produced, the court of the Norman King of Sicily, Roger II (1130–54), formed a crossroads at which Greek, Latin and Arabic cultures met. The Psalms had been translated into Arabic from Greek by al-Antaki of Antioch a century earlier. This trilingual Psalter was probably used at the royal chapel in Christian services. On this page the marginal inscription in Arabic marks Psalm 81 (in modern numbering) as that to be said on Fridays in line with the practice of the Latin church.

72 Psalm 81 (80), in Greek, Latin and Arabic
The Harley Trilingual Psalter
Palermo, Italy
between 1130 and 1154
315 x 230 mm
Harley MS 5786, f. 106v

86

73 Evangelist portrait of Matthew
Four Gospels
Constantinople
2nd quarter of 12th century (image)
220 x 170 mm
Burney MS 19, f. 1v

Prefacing his Gospel, Matthew is portrayed composing it, holding a pen and book, and seated at a desk with various writing implements. His name in Greek is written on the gold background. The image was inserted into a 10th-century Greek Gospel book, making it a more luxurious copy, perhaps for a member of the imperial court. Evangelist portraits underlined the authority of the Gospels, their basis in classical author portraits serving to legitimize and authenticate the text.

The complex and sophisticated layout of this Gospel Lectionary – one of only four known surviving Greek manuscripts with the text written entirely in the shape of a cross – suggests that it was made in the imperial scriptorium. The text pages include notation above each line, enabling the readings to be chanted. In addition, three important feasts have a title page like this one in which the cross shape is further embellished by a decorated frame.

74 Title page for readings for Pentecost from Matthew, in Greek
The London Cruciform Lectionary
Constantinople
12th century
370 x 280 mm
Add. MS 39603, f. 42

75 Portrait of Isaiah
The Siegburg Lectionary
Siegburg, Germany
2nd quarter of 12th century
270 x 160 mm
Harley MS 2889, f. 3v

This rare illustrated Latin Lectionary with readings from the Epistles is prefaced by an image of Isaiah. Labelled as a prophet, he holds a scroll with his messianic prophecy of Isaiah 11:1 ('A shoot will come up from the stump of Jesse'), regarded as a reference to Christ. It was written and decorated for the Benedictine abbey of Siegburg, near Cologne, and belongs to a group of manuscripts in a style that has clear connections to contemporary metalwork made in the same region.

Only eleven leaves are preserved of a small Latin Psalter made for Henry the
Lion, Duke of Saxony, and his English wife Matilda (married 1168, d. 1189).
Its prefatory images incorporate biblical passages, as here, where the
scrolls bear quotations from Exodus 13:2 (cited in Luke 2:23), describing
the consecration of the firstborn male to the Lord, and from Malachi 3:1,
regarding the coming of the Lord. Both foreshadow the Presentation above.

76 Presentation,
Moses and Malachi
The Psalter of Henry the Lion
Helmarshausen, Germany
between 1168 and 1189
210 x 130 mm
Lansdowne MS 381, part 1, f. 8

77 Virgin and Child
The Shaftesbury Psalter
Dorset ?, England
2nd quarter of 12th century
220 x 130 mm
Lansdowne MS 383, f. 165v

Entries in the calendar preceding this Latin Psalter, which includes an image of a woman, possibly the donor, in prayer before the Virgin and Child, connect it to the largest nunnery in England, at Shaftesbury in Dorset. In the early Middle Ages, Psalters were the most common prayer book used by literate men and women who could afford them. The relatively small size of this impressive copy is consistent with its probable use in the private devotions of the woman who commissioned it.

This large leaf, which originally prefaced a Psalter, is one of four that together form the longest sequence of New Testament illustrations produced in the 12th century. Narrating events from Christ's life, the detail shows events surrounding his birth: the Annunciation to the Shepherds, the Magi seeing the star and coming to Herod, their journey to visit the Christ Child, their Adoration of the Child, bearing gifts, their dream, the Presentation and Joseph's dream.

78 Scenes from the Life of Christ
Leaf from a Psalter
Canterbury, England
middle of 12th century
405 x 300 mm
Add. MS 37472, f. 1 (detail)

79 Christ in Majesty
Genesis, in Latin
The Parc Abbey Bible
Parc, near Leuven, southern Netherlands,
1148
430 × 305 mm
Add. MS 14788, f. 6v

A characteristic monastic production, this Bible was made for the
Premonstratensian abbey of St Mary in Parc (part of an order of canons
founded in 1120 by St. Norbert at Prémontré). The first word of Genesis, IN,
has been designed as a full-page monogram. Christ sits at the centre, labelled
as the A(lpha) and ω(Omega), the first and last letters of the Greek alphabet.
In the roundel below him, Abel offers his sacrifice, while at the top of the
page the dove of the Holy Spirit descends towards Christ.

The Latin text of the Gospel of Luke appears in two columns on the right portion of the page, written in a medieval Gothic script. The text is largely illegible as plain transcription due to the heavy abbreviation and paleographic conventions of the 12th-century manuscript.

Each of the Gospels in this Bible, made for the Premonstratensian abbey of Floreffe, begins with an allegorical composition comparing events related in the Old Testament to those of the New. Here an animal sacrifice prefigures the Crucifixion, as made explicit by the text inscribed on the arch: 'that Christ is the calf this *titulus* teaches'. Luke, to the right of the sacrifice, holds his symbol and a quotation from his Gospel (15:22).

80 Crucifixion, a sacrifice
Luke, in Latin
The Floreffe Bible
Meuse valley, southern Netherlands
middle or 3rd quarter of 12th century
475 x 330 mm
Add. MS 17738, f. 187

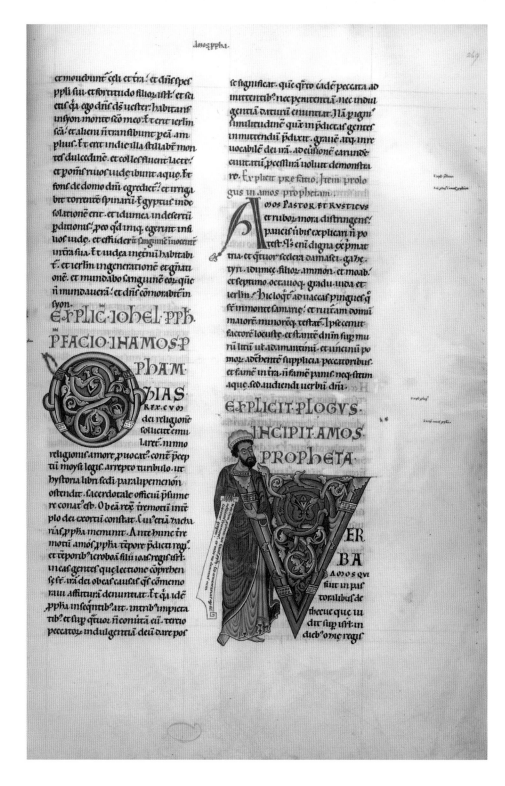

81 Portrait of Amos
Amos, in Latin
The Worms Bible
Frankenthal, near Worms, Germany
middle or 3rd quarter of 12th century
535 x 355 mm
Harley MS 2803, f. 269

The Bibles shown on these facing pages, like those on the preceding ones (figs. 79–80) are all enormous and contain the entire Vulgate text, in one or more volumes. They are representative of 12th-century monastic Bibles made for communal use. Like most Vulgate Bibles, they include a short prologue or introduction written by Jerome before each of the books. Here the preface has a decorated initial, while at the beginning of the book Amos clasps the first letter V(erba) (Words) in one hand, and a quotation from it (7:14) in the other.

The scale of these monastic Bibles (figs. 79–82) suggests that they would have been used to provide readings during services or meals. Given the elaborate nature of the decoration in this one, made at the abbey of St Mary and St Nicholas in Arnstein, the former use is more likely. The New Testament opens with an elaborate decoration of the first word *Liber* (Book) and a portrait of Matthew writing out this word on a parchment sheet.

82 Evangelist portrait of Matthew
Matthew, in Latin
The Arnstein Bible
Arnstein, near Koblenz, Germany
c. 1172
545 x 375 mm
Harley MS 2799, f. 155

eati immaculati in via: qui ambulant in lege domini.

Beati qui scrutantur testimonia eius: in toto corde exquirunt eum. Non enim qui operantur iniquitatem: in viis eius ambulaverunt. ❡ficationes tuas. Tu mandasti mandata tua: custodiri nimis. Utinam dirigantur vie mee: ad custodiendas iustificationes tuas. Tunc non confundar cum perspexero in omnibus mandatis tuis. ❡ et iudicia iustitie tue. Confitebor tibi in directione cordis mei: quod didici Iustificationes tuas custodiam: non me derelinquas usquequaque. Beth.   tibi.

IN quo corrigit adolescentior viam suam: in custodiendo sermones tuos. ❡mandatis tuis. In toto corde meo exquisivi te: ne repellas me a In corde meo abscondi eloquia tua: ut non peccem Benedictus es domine: doce me iustificationes tuas.

83 Christ and the Blessed,
Psalm 119 (118), in Latin
La Charité Psalter
La Charité-sur-Loire, France
last quarter of 12th century
255 x 160 mm
Harley MS 2895, f. 73v

Psalm 119 (118 in the Vulgate's numbering) begins with a description of the Blessed, who walk in the law of the Lord and keep his statutes. In this elegant Psalter the first letter of the word B(eati) (Blessed) includes an image of Christ holding open a scroll, perhaps representing the Lord's law being given to the Blessed. The Hebrew word *Beth* (the number 'two') is visible near the foot of the page at the second division of this Psalm, which starts with a large coloured letter.

This copy of the Psalms is 'glossed' with a commentary written in slightly smaller script around the central text. The initial for the first Psalm includes a visual commentary as well, in which David with his harp points upwards to Christ teaching a group of men; to the left a scroll identifies the resurrected Christ as the new Adam. The lower part of the letter is formed by a lion consuming a devil, who grasps a soul being rescued by an angel.

84 David and Christ
Psalm 1, in Latin
Glossed Psalter
Southern England or Northern France
middle of 12th century
260 x 175 mm
Add. MS 17392, f. 1

98

85 God blessing, man in waves
Psalm 69 (68), in Greek and Latin
The Holkham Bilingual Psalter
Paris
1st quarter of 13th century
280 x 195 mm
Add. MS 47674, f. 58v

The first line of Psalm 69 (68 in the numbering of the Vulgate, marked in
Roman numerals in the right margin of this manuscript) is, 'Save me, O God,
for the waters have come up to my neck'. Here the Latin version of this Psalm
is illustrated literally, with a man drowning in water, and God blessing above.
The parallel Greek text, which contains numerous mistakes, was probably
copied from a Greek manuscript by a French scribe. The decoration of the
initial Greek letter has been adapted to a Western style.

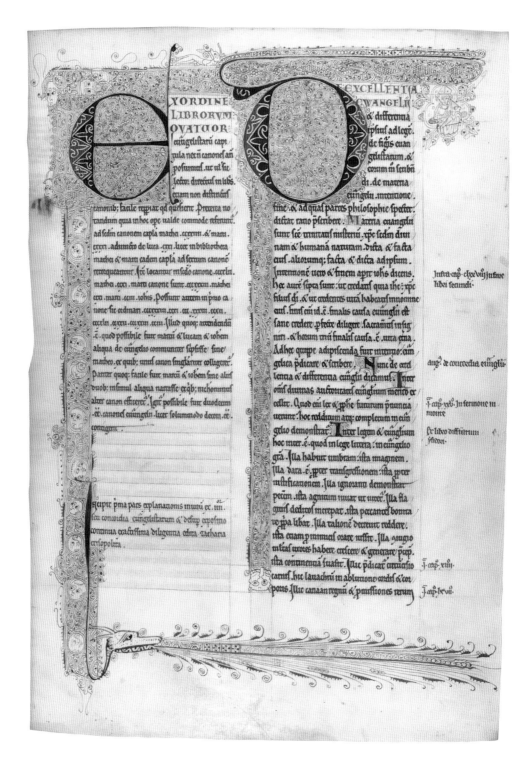

Various attempts have been made to harmonize or combine the Four Gospels into one unified account. This is a commentary written by Zacharias *Chrysopolitanus* (d. c. 1155) of Besançon (Chrysopolis) on an otherwise unknown Gospel Harmony. It is ornamented with elaborate penwork containing embedded faces and heads, and a small image of a bishop in the right margin, possibly intended as an author portrait.

86 Concordance, first chapter, in Latin
Zacharias Chrysopolitanus,
De concordia evangelistarum
Southern England
last quarter of 12th century or
1st quarter of 13th century
385 x 280 mm
Royal MS 4 D XII, f. 9

87 Portrait of Paul
1 Timothy, in Latin
Magna glossatura
Central or northern France
1st quarter of 13th century
445 x 290 mm
Royal MS 4 E IX, f. 164v

Peter Lombard (d. 1160), a teacher at the University of Paris, composed a commentary that became the standard text of biblical interpretation. As in this manuscript, his commentary was often copied alongside the biblical text in a carefully structured layout to facilitate study. A depiction of Paul seated and holding a scroll marks the opening of his Epistle. A slightly smaller gold letter begins the copy of Lombard's commentary, which is written to the right of the larger script of the biblical text.

In this extraordinary glossed study Bible the biblical text is written within a neat central rectangle, completely surrounded by symmetrically planned and spaced commentary. Each book opens with an image of its author (as here), or an illustration of its text, while each prologue and commentary begins with a decorated initial. Baruch, a disciple of Jeremiah, is traditionally regarded as the author of this deutero-canonical (or apocryphal) book of prophecy that formed part of the Vulgate translation of the Bible.

88 Portrait of Baruch
Baruch, in Latin
Glossed Bible
Paris
middle or 2nd half of 13th century
235 x 150 mm
Add. MS 16977, f. 177v

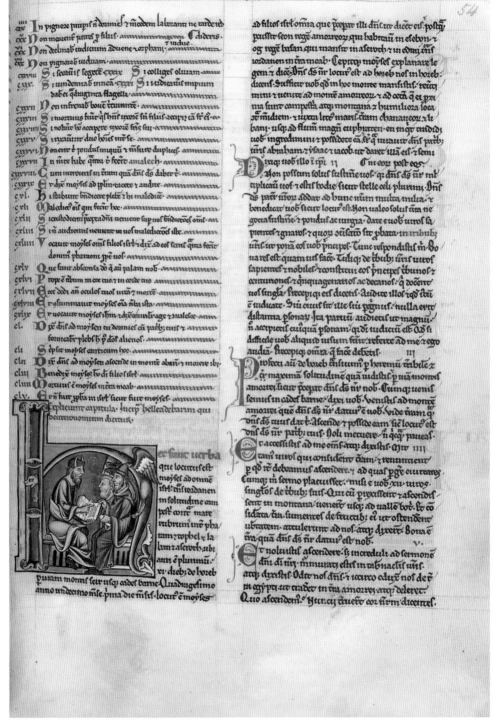

89 Moses speaking
Deuteronomy, in Latin
Bible
Paris ?
1st quarter of 13th century
210 x 150 mm
Add. MS 15452, f. 54

Deuteronomy begins, 'These are the words Moses spoke to all Israel in the wilderness'. In this elegant small portable Bible, the initial letter of the first word H([a]ec) is a literal illustration of this text, in which a seated Moses speaks from an open book and gestures to a group of listening Jews. As is common in medieval art, Moses is shown with horns because after his meeting with God on Mount Sinai his face became radiant, or in the Latin translation, cornutum, meaning 'shining' or alternatively, 'horned'.

Around the middle of the 12th century a university teacher in Paris, Peter Comestor (literally 'the Eater' because of his appetite for knowledge) (d. c. 1178) composed a short and readable biblical history narrating events, from Creation to the Acts of the Apostles. In this large copy, Numbers opens with a depiction of God speaking to Moses from the sky in the unusually brightly coloured landscape of Sinai. Moses holds open a long scroll, perhaps indicating the word of God that he was about to receive.

90 God appearing to Moses
Numbers, in Latin
Peter Comestor, Historia scholastica
Paris ?
1st half of 13th century
380 x 260 mm
Stowe MS 5, f. 46

91 Crucifixion
John 14:27–9; 15: 9–14
in Syriac
Syriac Lectionary
North-eastern Iraq
between 1216 and 1220
445 x 350 mm
Add. MS 7170, f. 151v

This very large and impressive Gospel lectionary is in Syriac, a dialect of Eastern Aramaic. An inscription in gold letters in the manuscript, naming particular abbots allows it to be dated. Its illustrations are closely related to another Lectionary, now in the Vatican, that was made at the monastery of Mar (saint in Aramaic) Mattai, near Mosul. Both are unusual amongst Syriac manuscripts for their inclusion of an extended narrative comprising scenes from the life of Christ.

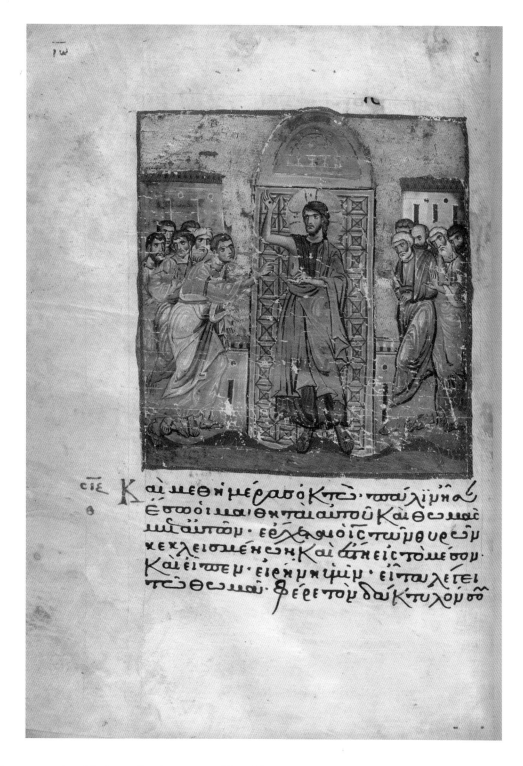

Whereas portraits of the Evangelists became a traditional feature of copies of the Gospels in Greek, narrative images were much less frequently included. This manuscript contains 17 narrative images of the life of Christ and of the saints, in addition to portraits of the Four Evangelists. Here Christ's invitation to Thomas to put his finger into the wound in Christ's side is illustrated directly above John's account of this event.

92 Incredulity of Thomas
John 20:26–27, in Greek
Four Gospels
Cyprus or Palestine
last quarter of 12th century
or first half of 13th century
225 x 165 mm
Harley MS 1810, f. 261v

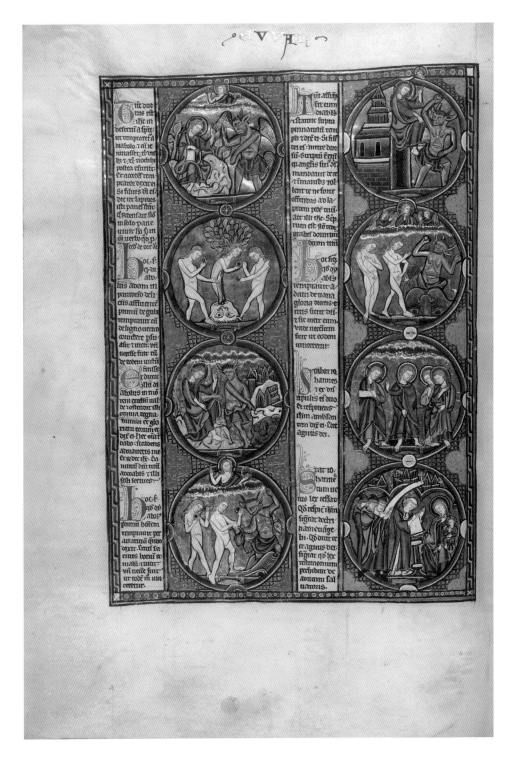

93 The Temptation and Fall,
Temptations in the Wilderness
Matthew 4:1–10, John 1:35–36, in Latin
Bible moralisée
Paris
2nd quarter of 13th century
400 x 275 mm
Harley MS 1527, f. 18v

Highly innovative in its use of the biblical text and focusing primarily on images, this manuscript is one of only seven similarly distinctive books that were made for the kings and queens of France and their closest relations. These manuscripts are called 'moralized Bibles' because each illustration is paired by another, here situated below the first, explaining in an allegorical sense its 'moral'. This arrangement occurs on every page, providing nearly 5000 images in a complete *Bible moralisée*.

Four pairs of facing pages at the beginning of this Latin copy of the Psalms present scenes from the life of Christ in an intricate pattern, reminiscent of stained glass. In the upper lobe to the left only Christ's feet are visible as he ascends into heaven – a composition apparently originating in England – while to the right the dove of the Holy Spirit descends on the Apostles. In the central lozenge Christ displays his wounds, and presides over the Last Judgment depicted in the lower lobes.

94 Ascension, Pentecost, Last Judgment
The Suneson Psalter
Paris
middle of 13th century
165 x 105 mm (shown at actual size)
Egerton MS 2652, f. 14

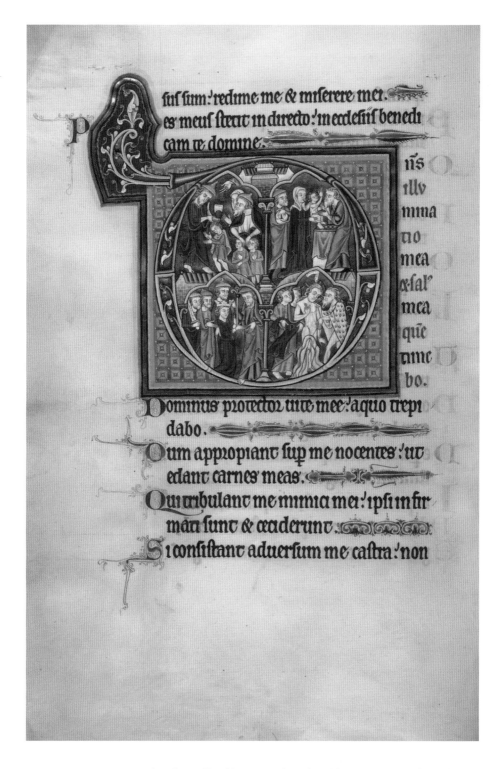

sus sum: redime me & miserere mei.

es meus stetit in directo: in ecclesiis benedi

cam te domine.

P

n̄s

illu

mina

tio

mea

& sal'

mea

quē

time

bo.

Dominus protector uite mee: a quo trepi

dabo.

Dum appropiant sup me nocentes: ut

edant carnes meas.

Qui tribulant me inimici mei: ipsi infir

mati sunt & ceciderunt.

Si consistant aduersum me castra: non

95 Anointing and Crowning of David,
Presentation, Baptism of Christ
Psalm 27 (26), in Latin
The York Psalter
England
3rd quarter of 13th century
345 x 240 mm
Add. MS 54179, f. 18v

The medieval interpretation of David as a 'type' or symbol of Christ is vividly illustrated in this extremely large initial D(omi)n[u]s (Lord), in which two scenes from David's life are paired with two from Christ's. In the upper pair David is anointed as King of Israel by the prophet Samuel with oil from a horn; to the right, Christ is presented in the Temple to Simeon, who prophesized that the child was 'a light for revelation to the Gentiles' (Luke 2:32). The lower pairing compares the crowning of David with the Baptism of Christ.

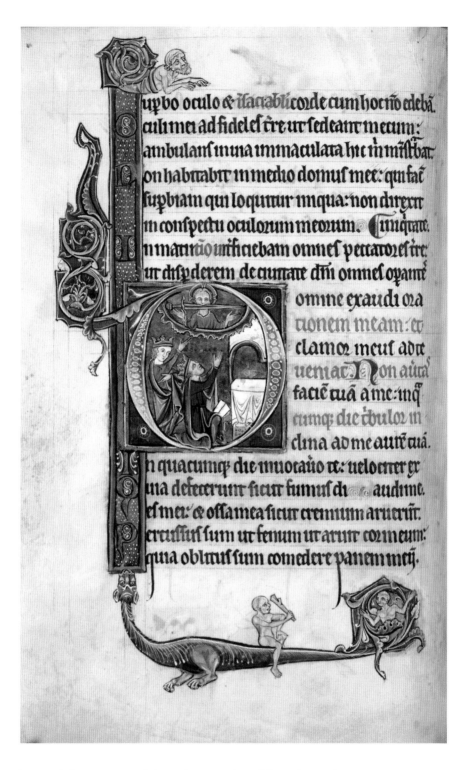

This initial also contains a Christian interpretation of the Psalm it illustrates, which includes the promise that the Lord will 'appear in his glory' (Psalm 102:16). Here a king in prayer (perhaps David) sees a vision of Christ with a sword in his mouth, a reference to Revelation 19 where 'a sharp sword' appears in the mouth of the 'Word of God'. This manuscript is better known, however, as the earliest surviving English example of a Psalter with extensive marginal imagery, much of which appears unconnected to the text.

96 David before God
Psalm 102 (101), in Latin
The Rutland Psalter
London ?
3rd quarter of 13th century
285 x 200 mm
Add. MS 62925, f. 99v

97 Creation
Genesis, in Latin
The Fécamp Bible
Paris
3rd quarter of 13th century
140 x 90 mm (shown at actual size)
Yates Thompson MS 1, f. 4v

Smaller than modern pocket paperbacks, the single-volume Bibles reproduced on these facing pages sharply contrast in size with earlier Bibles. Despite their different origins, both decorate the first letter of Genesis *I(n)* with roundels depicting the events of Creation. They demonstrate how the iconography, or subject matter, of illustrated initials could become standardized across Europe.

The shape of the first letter of Genesis I(n) offered medieval artists an opportunity to stretch it out to the length of a page, and to fill it with narrative imagery. The illustrations in each copy on these pages begin at the top of the letter with the creation of heaven and earth on the first day, followed by the creation of the firmament, the dry land and trees, the lights in the heavens, the animals and Eve (opposite) or Adam (above). The last image is of God's rest on the seventh day.

98 Creation
Genesis, in Latin
Pocket Bible
Bologna?, northern Italy
middle of 13th century
145 x 90 mm (shown at actual size)
Egerton MS 2908, f. 14

112

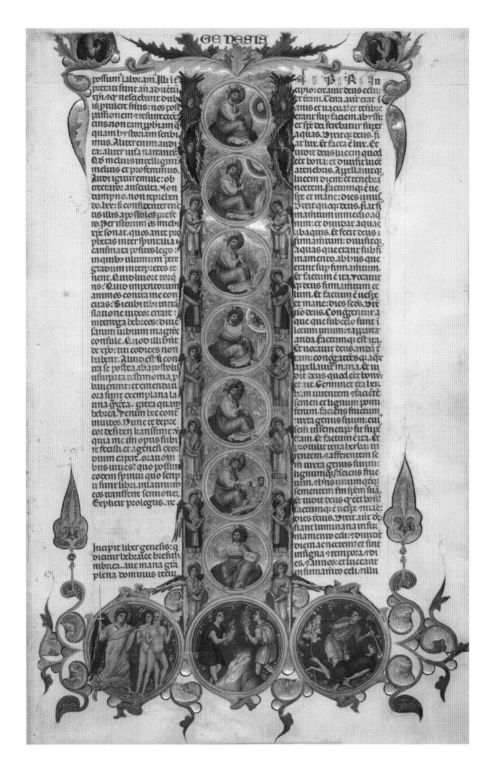

99 Creation, Expulsion, Cain and Abel
Genesis, in Latin
Bible
Bologna, Italy
last quarter of 13th century
385 x 250 mm
Add. MS 18720, Vol. I, f. 5

This large Italian Bible offered the artist even greater scope for illustrative possibilities than the smaller ones reproduced on the previous pages.
In addition to the Creation narrative, other episodes from Genesis are also included in the lower margin: the Expulsion from Paradise, Cain and Abel's Sacrifices, and the murder of Abel. Of the angels who flank the central roundels, the uppermost are red seraphim and blue cherubim with heads and wings only, who by tradition surround God in perpetual adoration.

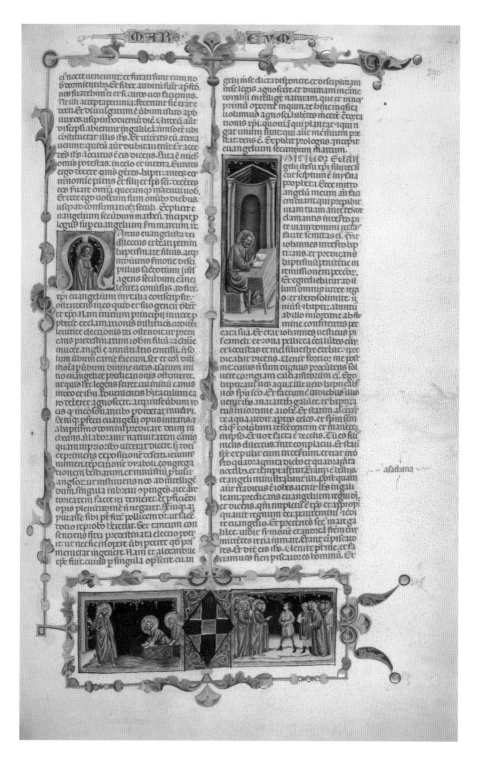

The decoration of this Bible, which also extends beyond the initial to the margins, includes depictions of several rarely illustrated episodes. At the beginning of Mark, the marginal scenes of Jesus walking on water towards his disciples in a boat (Mark 6:48–51), and casting out an unclean spirit complement Mark's portrait in the body of the text. The Bible was once owned by Robert of Geneva, the Anti-Pope Clement VII (elected 1378, d. 1394), from whom it takes its name.

100 Evangelist portrait of Mark,
Christ walking on water, casting out a devil
Mark, in Latin
The Bible of Clement VII
Naples, Italy
1st half of 14th century
360 x 245 mm
Add. MS 47672, f. 390

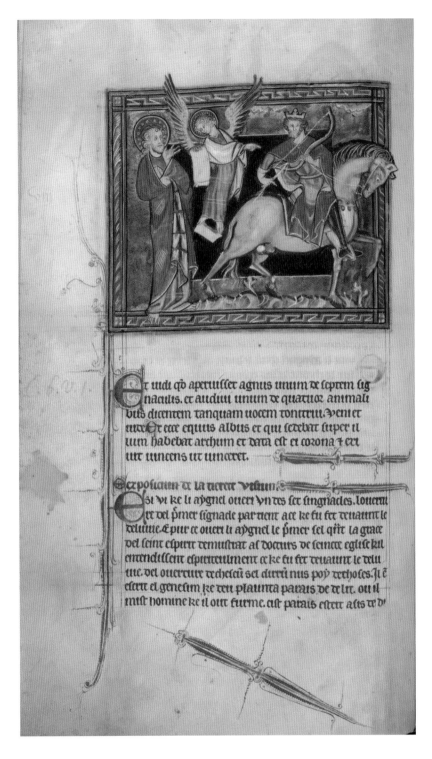

101 White horse of the Apocalypse
Revelation 6:1–2, in Latin and French
The Abingdon Apocalypse
Southern England
3rd quarter of 13th century
330 x 210 mm
Add. MS 42555, f. 11v

In England in the second half of the 13th century illustrated copies of the Apocalypse, or book of Revelation, became one of the most popular luxury books. This is the only surviving copy with a Latin text and French commentary where both are illustrated with large panels. The image on this page illustrates the biblical text. An angel points out to John the Evangelist, standing to the left, the first horseman of the Apocalypse who is mounted on a white horse with a bow and crown, going forth to conquer.

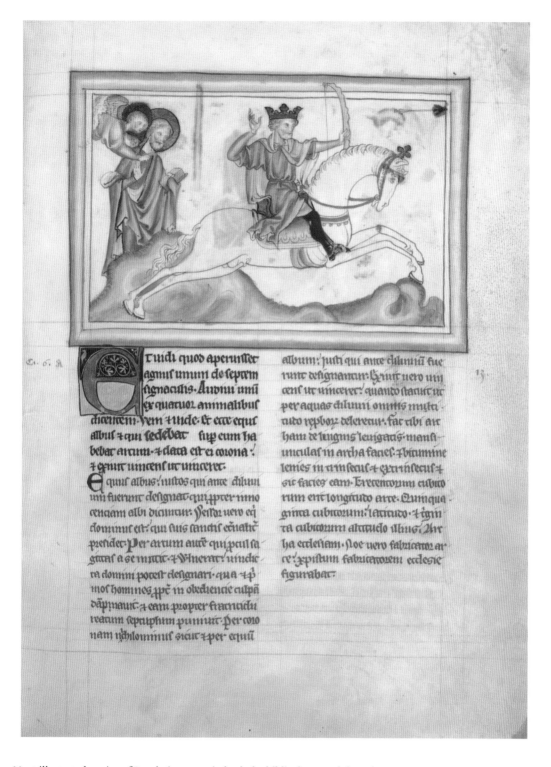

Most illustrated copies of Revelation contain both the biblical text and the commentary in Latin (the latter is here written in red). Like the *Abingdon Apocalypse* shown opposite, this copy includes a literal depiction of the first horseman of the Apocalypse, overlooked by John and the angel directing his attention. Here, however, the artist has used colour sparingly and less gold, and imbued both horse and rider with a sense of movement at the moment the horseman releases an arrow from his bow.

102 White horse of the Apocalypse
Revelation 6:1–2, in Latin
Apocalypse
London ?
3rd quarter of 13th century
290 x 220 mm
Add. MS 35166, f. 7

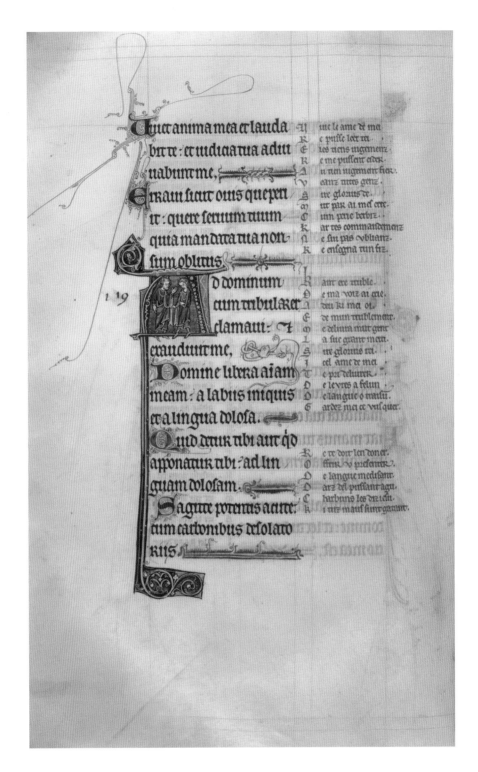

103 Moses and Aaron?
Psalm 120 (119), in Latin and French
The Oscott Psalter
Oxford ?, England
3rd quarter of 13th century
300 x 195 mm
Add. MS 50000, f. 189v

This manuscript is unusual because next to the Latin text is a translation of the Psalms in French verse. Both versions are carefully laid out, the parallel French written alternately in red or blue in groups of six short lines. Moses appears at the beginning of the group of Psalms (120–34), known as the Songs of Degrees or Ascent (or the Gradual Psalms), a title sometimes interpreted as an allusion to climbing the stairs of the Temple. Moses has been placed here, perhaps as a reference to his ascent of Mount Sinai to meet God.

durable beneurte que li nombre de.c. sene
tie. Ioleph fu en oint doingnemenz. Lame est
beneurte qui est en oince doingnemement de
uertu. z tant come ele uit ou cozf doit ele
estre tendie amie pardurable poz auencier
foi touz iozz abien faire. Se ele est guidee
en fon en esperance. z en charite ele de feruua
auenir par la grace ihesucrist a lesperance de
la deuine contemplacion de quoi est qui uiuent
ont pardurable leesce de quoi len lit: tu ma
empliras de leesce o ton uoust. Exodus

E sunt les nons des filz
israel qui entrerent o
iacob en egypte. Touz
ientrerent o toutes
leur mesnies. Ruben.
Symeon. Leui. Iudas.
ysachar. Zabulon. bin
iamin. Dan. z Neptalim.
Gad. z Aser. Contre les ames de ceus qui
issirent de la cuisse iacob estoient. lxx. z ioseph
estoit en egypte. z quant il fu mort. z sel fre
res touz. Li filz israel crurent autresi come se
il germassent. z monteplierent. z enforcierent
moult. z emplirent la terre. Entre ces choses
unt.i. nouuiaus rois sus egypte qui ne con

noissoit une ioseph si dist a son pueple. veez
que li pueples des filz israel est plus grans. z
plus fort que nos. venez si les apreinons sage
ment que il ne soit montepliez. par auenture
que se bataille uenoit contre nos. que il ne
se meissent o nos ennemis. z quant nos serio
uainu. si sen istroit de la terre. Il leur baila
loift mestres doingnurnes qui leur feissent fer
peter. z firent a pharaon citez z tabernacles.
Phytom. z Ramesses. z de tant plus les apremo
ent. z il plus monteplioient. z cressoient. Cil
degypte haoient les filz israel. z les tormen
toient. z les gauoient. z en auoient enuie.
z leur feseient mener amere uie par dures
oeures de boe. z de tuilles. z de touz le feruise
dont il euent apreint es ouuraignes de terre.
li rois degypte dist aus fames uenterieres aus
ebreues dont lune auoit non Sepham. z lau
tre phua. si leur comanda quant les fames
ebreues deuront enfanter. z nos uerrois se li
enfes est males occiez le. se ce est fame lessiez
la. Les uenterieus crenurent dumedieu. z ne
firent pas les comandement autoi degypte
ains guidoient les masles. li rois les apela z
leur dist. quest ce que uos auez. sur que nos
auez lessiez les enfanz masles. Eles li respondi
rent. sire. les fames ebraïeus ne sunt pas come
celes degypte. Eles meisnes sune uenterieres
z ont enfante ainz que nos uaingnons a eus.
diex sit bien aus uenterieus. z li pueples crut
z fu confortez. z porce que les uenterieus cre
mirent dieu il leur edefiamaisons. Pharaon
comanda a tout son pueple. z dist touz les mal
les qui nestront gitez en.i. fleuue. z les fa
mes guidez. II

pres ce issi uns home de la mesnice leui.
z prist fame de sa lignie. z conceut z or
.i. filz. z quant ele uit quil fu moult biaus
ele le repost par.iij. moiz. z quant ele ne le
pot plus celer ele prist une huche de ions. z

Translations of the entire Bible into vernacular languages were rare in
the Middle Ages. This manuscript in French is one of only three known
surviving copies of an early French translation of the Vulgate made before
the completion of the more common paraphrase, the *Bible historiale*,
at the end of the 13th century. This copy is also richly decorated, with
both an illustration of the book and a narrative or decorated initial
in gold at the beginning of each biblical book.

104 Moses and Jews
Exodus, in French
Bible
Paris
last quarter of 13th century
400 x 290 mm
Harley MS 616, f. 53

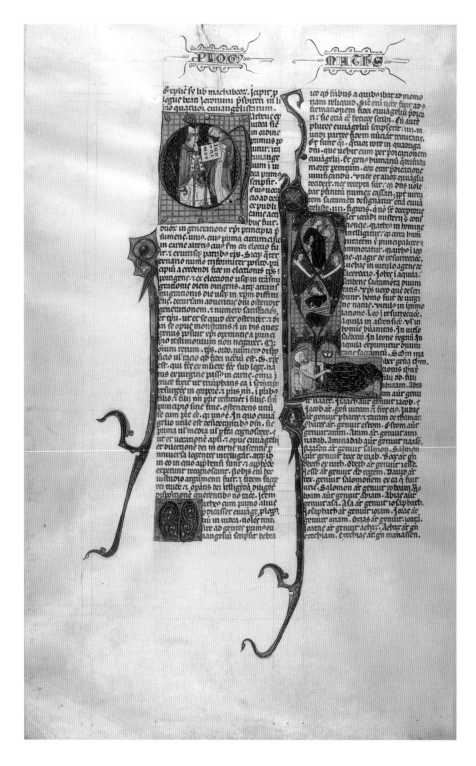

105 Tree of Jesse
Matthew, in Latin
The Poncii Bible
Catalonia, Spain
1273
380 x 255 mm
Add. MS 50003, f. 364v

A prophecy from Isaiah 11 states that a messiah would spring from the root or family of Jesse, the father of David. In many Christian Bibles this prophecy forms the subject of the illustrations placed at the beginning of Matthew's Gospel, and preceding his genealogy of Jesus. Typically, the ancestors of Jesus, such as David, are depicted. Unusually here, in the initial L(iber), the tree rising from the body of Jesse includes haloed musicians and figures clasping scrolls.

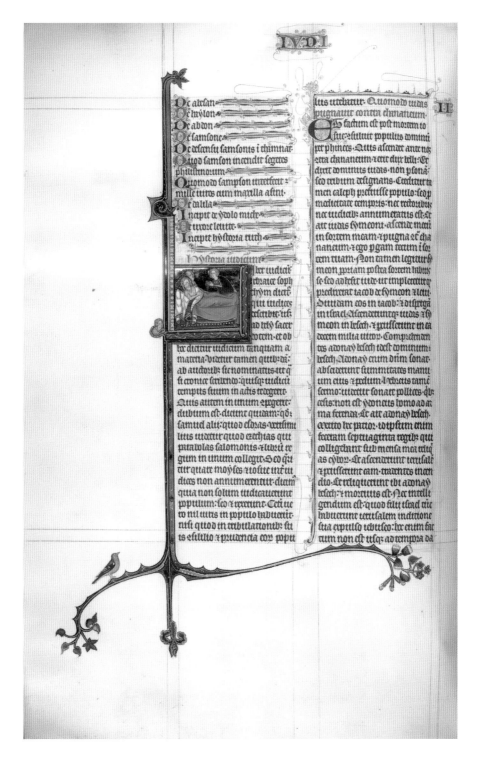

Peter Comestor's biblical history remained a popular text throughout the Middle Ages, and many luxury copies of it survive. Like contemporary Bibles, the books of this *Historia scholastica* include illustrated initials, and bar borders with sprouting foliage and marginal figures characteristic of English art of the period. As in the Bible opposite, the initial L illustrated (in this case with the death of Joshua), is the first of the Latin word *Liber* (Book). The first lines of Judges tell of events after the death of Joshua, who died aged 110.

106 Death of Joshua
Judges, in Latin
The Ashridge Comestor
London ?
between 1283 and 1300
400 x 265 mm
Royal MS 3 D VI, f. 104v

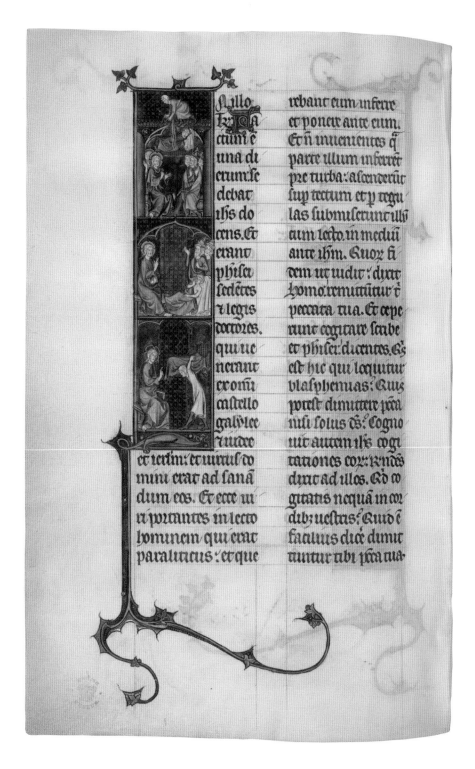

107–108 Healing of a paralytic, Luke 5:17–23; Raising of Jairus's daughter, Matthew 9:18–19, in Latin
Gospel Lectionary
Paris
last quarter of 13th century
310 x 200 mm
Add. MS 17341, ff. 98v, 134

This manuscript is an exact copy of an earlier 13th-century Lectionary made for the Sainte-Chapelle in Paris, apparently produced while the model was in loose leaves prior to its rebinding. Because almost all of the Gospel readings for the liturgical year are illustrated in it, the volume provides a complete sequence of scenes from the life of Christ. These include many rarely depicted events, such as (left) the lowering of a paralytic into a room where Jesus was

teaching, taking up three compartments of the I(n) of the introduction *In illo tempore* (in that time). On the right, the Raising of Jairus's daughter is treated even more elaborately, taking the whole height of the text to show Jairus's entreaty to Christ to raise his dead daughter, his lamenting household, Christ's approach, and the resurrection of the girl.

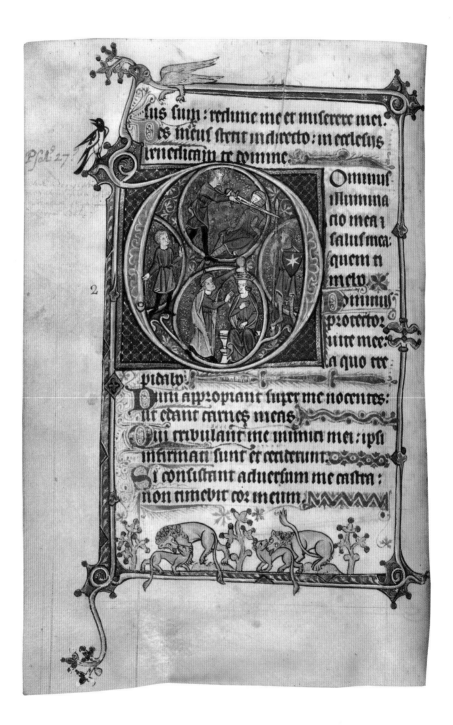

109 Slaying of Goliath, Anointing of David
Psalm 27 (26), in Latin
The Percy Psalter
York ?, England
last quarter of 13th century
175 x 110 mm (shown at actual size)
Add. MS 70000, f. 39v

Although they were made in different countries, both of the Psalters on these pages illustrate the beginning of Psalm 26 (in the Vulgate's numbering) with an image of the Anointing of David by Samuel. This imagery became standard in illustrated copies of the Psalms, inspired by the Psalm's title, 'The Psalm of David before he was anointed', even though the title itself is often not included. This English copy includes another important scene from David's life: his battle with Goliath.

Psalm 26 marked the second major division of the Psalms, starting the group that was to be read on Mondays. Like most Psalters, this copy also includes a litany of prayers to various saints. This manuscript includes Breton saints in its list, indicating that it was probably made for use in Brittany. It was later owned by King Henry VIII (1509–47). In addition to large narrative initials with traditional subjects, there is a bright animal or imaginary creature decorating the lower margin of virtually every page.

110 Anointing of David
Psalm 27 (26), in Latin
Psalter
Paris ?
last quarter of 13th century
215 x 145 mm
Yates Thompson MS 18, f. 35v

111 Men bowing to the dragon
Revelation 13, in French
Apocalypse in French
Southern England
1st quarter of 14th century
290 x 190 mm
Add. MS 38842, f. 5

The two Apocalypses on these pages, which each contains the text of Revelation and a commentary on it in French, indicate the continued popularity of illustrated copies of the text, presumably amongst lay people. Kneeling and talking men before a dragon illustrate literally Revelation 13:4, in which John recounts how men worshiped the dragon, and questioned each other about the beast.

In this copy of Revelation each biblical chapter is summarized and followed by a commentary explaining the text in simple terms. A large illustration precedes each chapter. When the last seal of the book of seven seals is opened, seven angels appear. On the left, the fifth angel opens the Abyss, from which emerge locusts that 'looked like horses' and whose 'faces resembled human faces' (Revelation 9:7). On the right the sixth angel frees the angels that are bound in the river Euphrates (Revelation 9:14).

112 Fifth and Sixth trumpets
Revelation 9–10, in French
The Huth Apocalypse
Northern or central France
1st quarter of 14th century
280 x 195 mm
Add. MS 38118, f. 16

Oe coment il chapentoist Por uessel q dieu disoist E au tensnel
puit chener. Si uinnt dieu por luy enseigner. E dint noee: ore tes
chance tot. Noe le acudoist ne sona mot. Pren de uerges si les sace au
Car le repeste est enuenaunt. Deux adunk thidelur pfirt. E le uessel.
Noe cheuirt. le uessel il mist ben a fere. Secu cent aune ii deuonisu
il furout apreste a home estoist la Arke noe. De turt bestes deten il u
male femele ceo dut lescript. E de turt ofseus une pire. De tur culur
blauche negrit. E sa feme ses enfauntr. E hur femes ofseus potauir
E quint ele estoist de tur charge la ewe uint cumnt agraut plent

113–114 *Noah building the Ark, Sending out
the raven and dove*
The Holkham Bible Picture Book
London ?
2nd quarter of 14th century
285 x 210 mm
Add. MS 47682, ff. 7v-8

Within the unique sequence of illustrations preserved in this manuscript,
apocryphal episodes and details drawn from late medieval life have been
woven into a biblical narrative extending from Creation to the Last Judgment.
The Dominican friar for whom it was made, perhaps as a teaching aid for the
rich and powerful, is depicted at the opening of the volume instructing the
artist: 'Now do it well and thoroughly, for it will be shown to important

people'. To help in his instruction the illustrations are accompanied by brief explanatory texts in Anglo-Norman French, the literary language most familiar to contemporary English nobles. Separate episodes are sometimes conflated in a single illustration: for example, the dove at the left of the right-hand page is seen being released by Noah, finding an olive branch, and returning with it in its mouth.

115 Baptism of Christ, David playing bells
Psalm 81 (80), in Latin
The Queen Mary Psalter
London ?
1st quarter of 14th century
275 x 175 mm
Royal MS 2 B VII, f. 190v

One of the most lavishly illustrated biblical manuscripts produced in England, and later owned by Queen Mary Tudor (1553–58), this Psalter contains around 1,000 images. Prefacing, commenting on, and embellishing the Psalms, the illustrations are justly famous for their artistic sophistication in different media – both coloured drawings and paintings. On this page, in the initial beneath the Baptism, King David plays the bells, illustrating the beginning of the Psalm, 'Sing for joy to God our strength; shout aloud to the God of Jacob!'.

Psalm 109 is the last of the eight-part Psalm divisions used in the Divine Office, this group being said at Vespers on Sunday evenings. Often, as here, in the initial D(ixit), it was decorated with an image of the Trinity, corresponding to the Christian interpretation of its opening lines: 'The Lord said to my Lord: Sit thou at my right hand.' The volume was once owned by the antiquary Lord William Howard (1563–1640).

116 Trinity
Psalm 110 (109), in Latin
The Howard Psalter
London
1st quarter of 14th century
355 × 230 mm
Arundel MS 83 [I], f. 72

117–118 Trinity
Psalm 110 (109), in Latin
The Gorleston Psalter
East Anglia, England
1st quarter of 14th century
375 x 235 mm
Add. MS 49622, ff. 146v-147

This manuscript was written and decorated for someone of considerable wealth who had connections with the church of St Andrew in Gorleston, near Yarmouth: the dedication of the church is mentioned in the calendar. It is a central work in a group of manuscripts produced for East Anglian patrons in the first quarter of the 14th century, and demonstrates

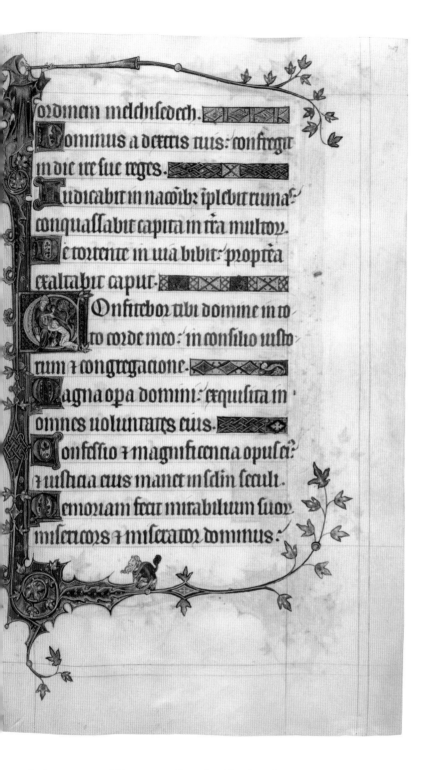

the importance of this East Anglian school in a broader perspective as one of the high points of English art. Its decoration includes many marginal scenes and figures, ranging in subject from sacred to profane, and including creatively imagined hybrid creatures and humorous vignettes in which animals feature prominently.

119 Trinity, Last Supper
Reading for Corpus Christi, in Latin
Sainte-Chapelle Epistle Lectionary
Paris
2nd quarter of 14th century
410 x 285 mm
Yates Thompson MS 34, f. 116v

Made in Paris, this Lectionary had its readings from the Bible almost immediately adapted for the use of the Sainte-Chapelle, the chapel built by Louis IX (1226–70) in the royal palace in Paris. The elegant initials, both of which are framed within bar borders characteristic of the period, illustrate the text and clearly mark the beginning of each reading. On this page the readings from 2 Corinthians 13:13 and 1 Corinthians 11:23 both begin with the word *Fratres* (brothers).

The *Bible historiale* consists of a French translation of the Bible with interpolated passages from the work of the 12th-century scholar Peter Comestor. This beautiful copy was made for the French King Jean II le Bon (1350–64) before he was captured at the battle of Poitiers and taken to England as a prisoner. The upper scenes illustrate Solomon teaching his son, Rehoboam (left) and the Judgement of Solomon (right). In the lower scenes, Solomon tests an inheritance dispute by asking the three rivals to shoot an arrow at their father's corpse.

120 Solomon teaching Rehoboam, Judgment of Solomon, Solomon deciding an inheritance dispute
Proverbs, in French
Bible historiale (complétée moyenne) of Jean le Bon
Paris
between 1350 and 1356
420 x 285 mm
Royal MS 19 D II, f. 273

121 Luke, in Serbian
The Gospels of Jakov of Serres
Serres, Serbian Empire
1354
310 x 225 mm
Add. MS 39626, f. 145

This copy of the Four Gospels in Serbian Church Slavonic is one of the finest books produced within the empire of Stefan Uroš IV Dušan (1331–55). Its illumination, including the ornamental panel at the beginning of Luke, derives from Byzantine models. The large Cyrillic letter written in red in the right-hand margin gives the pericope number, which identifies the time during the liturgical year at which this passage from Luke's Gospel would be read.

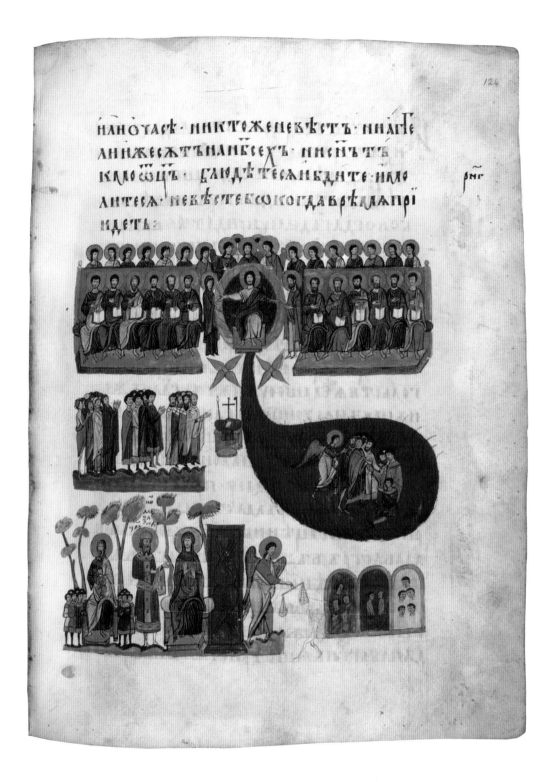

НАНОТАСЄ · НІКТОЖЕПЕВѢСТЪ · НІАГГЄ
ЛІ НІЖЄСѪТЪ НАНБЄСЕХЪ · НІСНѪТЪ
КАІО ѠЦЪ · ГАІ ДѢТЄ АНБДІТЄ · НІМО
ЛІТЄ СА · НЕВѢСТЄ БО КОГДА ВРѢЛАПРІ
ИДЕТЪ ·

This manuscript, the most celebrated surviving example of Bulgarian medieval art, contains a remarkable sequence of 366 illustrations of the life and teachings of Christ. The large image of the Last Judgment is prompted by the prophecy of Christ to his disciples in Mark's text. The illuminator's adoption of a Byzantine artistic model (here it includes a portrait of Tsar Ivan Alexander [1331–71] at the lower left) may have been a deliberate aesthetic choice to promote Bulgarian imperial ambitions.

122 Last Judgment
The Gospels of Tsar Ivan Alexander
Turnovo ?, Bulgaria
1355–56
330 x 240 mm
Add. MS 39627, f. 124

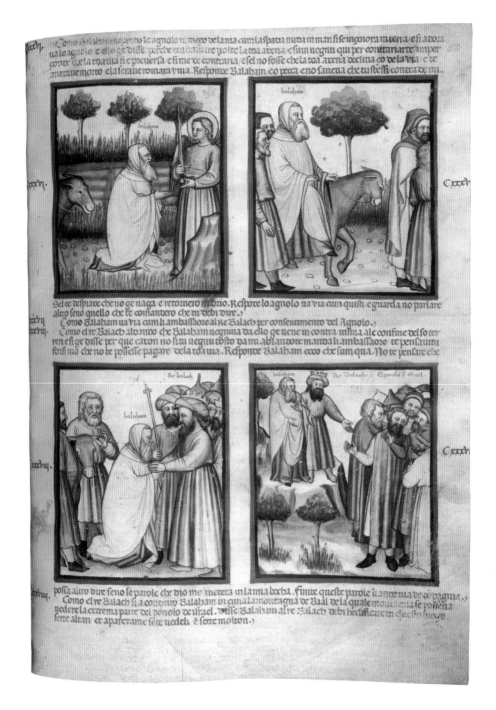

123 Balaam
Paduan Bible Picture Book
Padua ?, Italy
last quarter of 14th century
325 x 230 mm
Add. MS 15277, f. 50

Picture books of parts of the Old Testament with vernacular commentary were popular throughout the medieval period, and were produced probably for lay people. In this Italian example, illustrating the events described in Numbers 22–23, the first scene (upper left) illustrates the moment when Balaam's eyes are opened, and he sees 'the Angel of the Lord standing in the road with his sword drawn'. The Angel tells Balaam to continue his journey to Moab (upper right), where Balaam encounters King Balak and the Israelites (lower scenes).

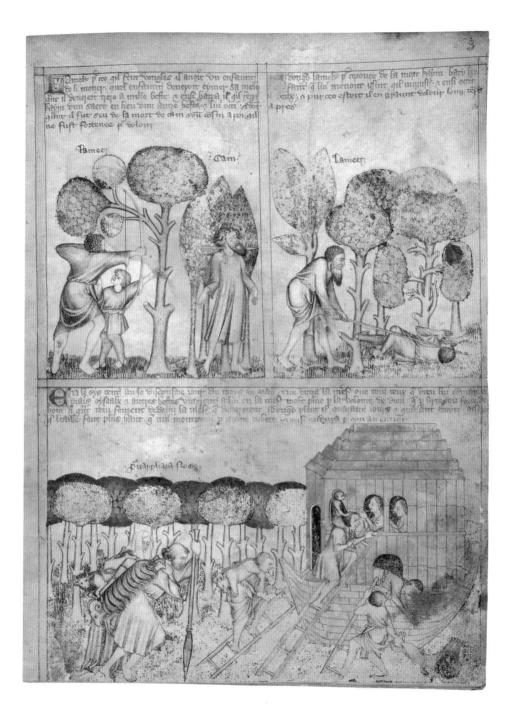

Together with 19 other leaves, this page forms part of a picture book of Genesis. The relative size of the illumination makes it a clear example of the primacy of image over text. In certain cases the captions in French written by an English scribe do not correspond with the scenes depicted. On this page the upper scenes illustrate an apocryphal story apparently derived from the *Historia scholastica*. The blind Lamech, guided by his son Tubal-cain, shoots Cain with an arrow by accident, and then kills his guide.

124 Lamech killing Cain, Tubal-cain, Noah's Ark
The Egerton Genesis
Southern England
3rd quarter of 14th century
245 x 195 mm
Egerton MS 1894, f. 3

125 Psalm 90 (89), in English and Latin
Psalter
England
1st quarter of the 15th century
380 x 255 mm
Royal MS 18 C XXVI, f. 1V

The first literal translation of the Psalms into English was made by Richard Rolle (1305/1310–49), a hermit and religious writer born in Yorkshire. His version pre-dates the more famous Wycliffite translation of the 1380s (fig. 126). Rolle completed the translation in order to enhance the understanding of the recitation of the Psalms by his closest disciple, the anchoress Margaret Kirkby (d. 1391–94). In this bilingual manuscript both the Latin and English biblical verses are underlined in red, and followed by a commentary in English.

This volume preserves the earliest securely datable copy of the complete Bible in English. Its text is the earlier version of the translation produced by followers of the Oxford teacher John Wycliffe (d. 1384); it is a word-for-word rendering of the Vulgate that sometimes distorts natural English word order. The ownership of this grand copy by Thomas Woodstock, Duke of Gloucester (1355–97), the youngest son of Edward III, indicates the high social level at which the new translation was initially accepted.

126 Isaiah, in English
Wycliffite Bible
London
before 1397
440 x 300 mm
Egerton MS 617, f. 54

127 Samson, Resurrection, Jonah
Biblia pauperum
The Hague ?, northern Netherlands
c. 1405
175 x 385 mm
King's MS 5, f. 20

In the *Biblia pauperum* (Bible of the poor) a sequence of depictions of scenes from the life of Christ is linked to Old Testament subjects regarded as their prefigurations, a comparative device known as typology. Typically, one Old Testament 'type' is drawn from the time before Moses, or before the Law, and the other from the time after Moses, or under the Law. This lavish example demonstrates that the work's modern title could be a misnomer. It may have

legit ione cap̃ ſcd̃ .
Quod cũ ipe ionas,
fuſſet in uentre cetı
tribus dieb; et tribz
noctibus poſtea piſ
as eum erpuıt ſup
terram arıdam . Jo
nas quı poſt tres dıes
eriuıt de pıſce fıgura
bat rp̃m qui poſt tres
dıes de ſepulcro eri
uıt et reſurrexıt.

been made for a member of the court at The Hague, Margaret of Cleves (d. 1411), the second wife of Albrecht, Duke of Bavaria and Count of Holland, and its accompanying Latin explanations are written entirely in gold, red, or blue. Here Samson's escape from the Philistines (he is seen carrying the gates from the city of Gaza in the left-hand image), and Jonah's deliverance from the belly of the whale (on the right) prefigure the central image of Christ's Resurrection.

128 Trinity, Evangelists with their symbols
Matthew, in French
Bible historiale (complétée) of Charles of France
Paris
c. 1420
460 x 330 mm
Add. MS 18857, f. 148

The heraldic arms inserted at the beginning of each volume of this sumptuous French history Bible indicate that it was owned by a French prince, probably Charles of France, the younger brother of King Louis XI, when he was Duke of Normandy between 1465 and 1469. At the beginning of the Gospels the Evangelists and their symbols surround an image of the Trinity, in which the Holy Spirit appears as a dove.

The 'pearl' of the manuscript copies of Guyart des Moulins's French translation of a Bible history is this manuscript, signed by its scribe, Thomas du Val. The manuscript is of special importance because it contains portions of des Moulins's compilation that are replaced by the biblical text in other copies. The beginning of Proverbs, a book traditionally ascribed to Solomon, is illustrated by an enthroned Solomon, instructing his son Rehoboam, flanked by courtiers in contemporary medieval dress.

129 Solomon, Rehoboam and courtiers
Proverbs, in French
Bible historiale (early version)
Paris
1411
445 x 340 mm
Royal MS 19 D III, Vol. 2, f. 289

130 Job feasting; on a dunghill
Job, in Latin
The Great Bible
London ?
1st quarter of 15th century
625 x 430 mm
Royal MS 1 E IX, f. 136v (detail)

With 143 illustrated initials, this vast Bible contains the last extensive biblical sequence in English manuscript production. It may be the 'Great Bible' that once belonged to King Henry IV (1399–1413). The opening initial of Job, which is in two parts, shows Job's life before and after his affliction: first, feasting with his family, his ermine gown highlighting his great wealth; then below, naked on a dunghill illustrating his comment, 'Naked I came from my mother's womb, and naked I will depart' (Job 1:21).

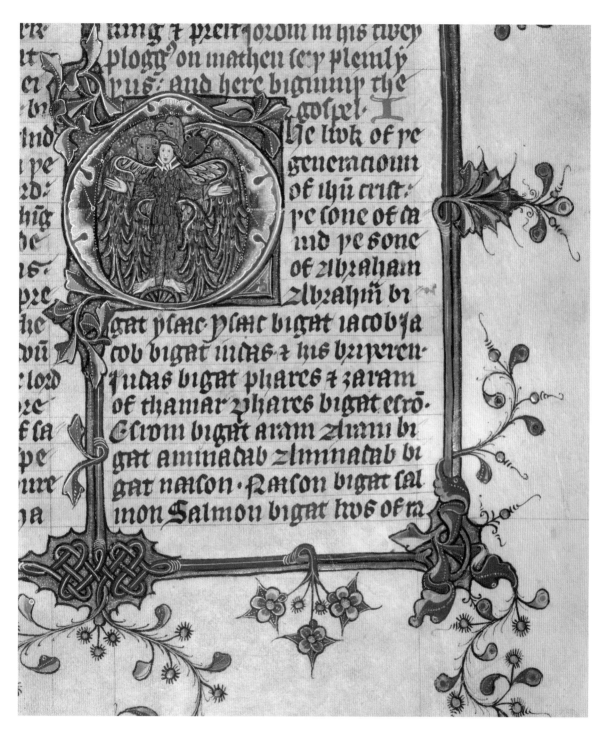

Within around ten years the somewhat stilted language of the 'early' literal
Wycliffite translation was completely revised. This revision, the 'later'
Wycliffite version, followed the structure of Middle English rather than that
of Latin, resulting in a more fluid translation. This copy of the later version
includes an unusual illustrated initial T(he) at the beginning of the New
Testament in which the symbols of the four Evangelists are incorporated into
a single body with four heads, stressing the unity of the Four Gospels.

131 Tetramorph
Matthew, in English
Wycliffite Bible
North Midlands, England
1st quarter of 15th century
405 x 255 mm
Arundel MS 104, Vol. 2, f. 251 (detail)

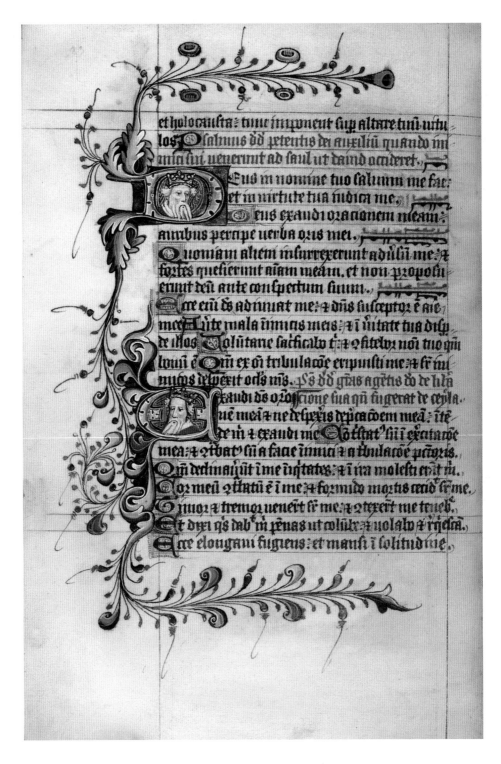

132 Psalms 54–55 (53–54), in Latin
The Psalter of Humfrey of Gloucester
London ?
2nd quarter of 15th century
245 x 165 mm
Royal MS 2 B I, f. 27v

This selection of Psalms was made for Humfrey, Duke of Gloucester (1414–47), the youngest son of King Henry IV and a renowned bibliophile. The nearly 50 Psalms included are preceded and followed by prayers, and together with a calendar and litany, they form a specialized prayer book. The beginning of each Psalm is marked by a decorated initial letter, most of which include a depiction of the head of a king. Each verse opens with a blue or gold initial.

The later Wycliffite translation was widely used, even though after 1407–09 a special licence from the local bishop was required in order to possess a copy of it. In this copy the Latin text of the Vulgate written in red is followed by the English translation in brown. The beginning of Psalm 27 is translated as: 'The Lord is my lightnyng and my helthe Whom shall y drede?'. The lush foliate decoration of the border, like that on the opposite page, is characteristic of English illumination of the period.

133 Psalm 27 (26), in English and Latin
Wycliffite Psalter
Southern England
middle of 15th century
285 x 210 mm
Harley MS 1896, f. 16

148

134 Elkanah and his wives
1 Samuel (I Kings), in Dutch
Flemish Bible History
Utrecht, northern Netherlands
2nd quarter of 15th century
390 x 285 mm
Add. MS 15410, f. 177v

Dutch painters illustrated several deluxe copies of a vernacular version of the Bible. Arguably the finest illustration in this history Bible shows Elkanah standing between his two wives, Peninnah and her children, and a weeping, childless Hannah. The same subject appears in the 12th-century Rochester Bible (fig. 69), but within an initial letter rather than as a separate image.

Copied by George Rörer of Regensburg in 1465, a year before the production of the first printed Bible in German, this German translation of the Old Testament is evidence of the continuing demand in the later Middle Ages for luxury copies of the Bible with traditional illustration. Here, at the beginning of the deutero-canonical book of Wisdom, Solomon is depicted hearing the case of two women, both of whom claim to be the mother of a baby. The second child in the image is the dead baby of one of the women.

135 Judgment of Solomon
Wisdom, in German
High German Old Testament
Regensburg, Germany
1465
380 x 280 mm
Egerton MS 1896, f. 60

Cōmt le roy pharaon songit deux muellaurs songez

136 Pharaoh's dream
Genesis Picture Book
Southern Netherlands or eastern France ?
last quarter of 15th century
265 x 190 mm
Add. MS 39657, f. 110v

Towards the end of the Middle Ages, Bible picture books were produced that had as their focus coloured line drawings, similar to the woodcuts that were appearing in printed books. Accompanied only by brief captions in French, the illustrations in this volume relate the biblical narrative with a bold directness. Here Pharaoh dreams of seven fat and seven lean cows that come out of the river, while on the bank only seven remain, the lean cows having consumed the fat ones, as recorded in Genesis 41:1–4.

This is a rare medieval copy of the Bible in Catalan. The decoration of the beginning of Genesis, shown here, is closely related to one of the other surviving copies, now in Paris. The Bible was first translated into Catalan as word-by-word rendering from the French, commissioned by King Alfonso II of Catalonia (III of Aragon) (1265–91). The text in this 15th-century copy is a translation from the Latin Vulgate, although it incorporates certain phrases and glosses from a French translation.

137 Creation
Genesis, in Catalan
Catalan Old Testament
Catalonia
1465
410 x 270 mm
Egerton MS 1526, f. 3

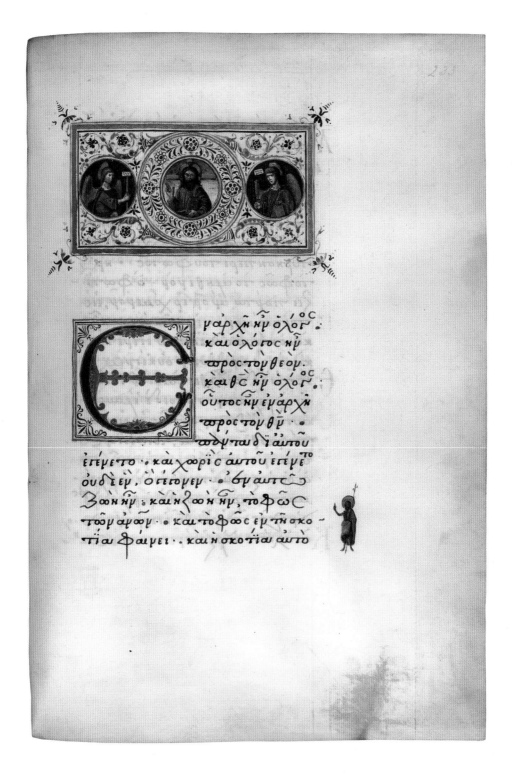

233

γ ἀρχ ῆν ὁ λό ꙋⲥ
και ο λό γος ἦ ν
πρὸς τὸν θεόν.
και θ̅ⲥ̅ ἦν ὁ λό γⲟⲥ.
ⲟὗτος ἦν ἐ μ ἀρχ ῆ
πρὸς τὸν θ̅ν̅
πάντα δ ι ἀυτοῦ
ἐ γ έ γε το · κ αι χ ωρὶ ς ἀυτοῦ ἐ γ έ
ⲟ ὐ δ ὲ ν · ὅ γ έ γονε · · ἐ ν ἀυτⲱ̅
3 ωὴ ἦ ν · κ αι ἡ ζω ὴ ἦ ν · τὸ φ ῶ ⲥ
τῶ ν ἀνθρώ πων · · κ αι τὸ φ ῶⲥ ἐ ν τῆ σκο -
τ ί ᾳ φ αίνει · · κ αι ἡ σκο τ ία ἀυτὸ

138 Christ blessing flanked by angels
John, in Greek
The Greek Gospels of Cardinal Gonzaga
Rome
1478
310 x 215 mm
Harley MS 5790, f. 233

Commissioned by Cardinal Francesco Gonzaga (d. 1483), this is a rare example of a luxury copy of the Four Gospels made in Greek for a Western patron. The Italian illuminator was apparently copying the imagery directly from a Byzantine exemplar. So, the beginning of the Gospel of John includes a headpiece, and a marginal figure of John the Baptist next to the verse that mentions him, both typically Byzantine details. However, the artist has painted these subjects in a Western style.

Traditional Byzantine forms of decorated headpieces and initials are interpreted in a non-Greek context in this copy of the Four Gospels in Church Slavonic. The beginning of each Gospel is marked by a full-page portrait of the Evangelist, framed in a panel of silk, and a decorated text page, as seen here. At the end of the book are tables that identify which passages from the Gospels are to be read on successive days of the year.

139 John, in Church Slavonic
Russian Gospels
Russia
c. 1500
190 x 140 mm
Egerton MS 3045, f. 233

140 Portrait of Matthew
Evangelist portrait
Rome
3rd quarter of 16th century
120 x 105 mm (shown at actual size)
Add. MS 49520

Probably once part of a Latin Gospel Lectionary made for the papal chapel in Rome, this finely executed image demonstrates the unbroken tradition of painting Evangelist portraits in deluxe manuscripts. In this Renaissance interpretation Matthew's symbol of a winged man has become a winged child or putto, tenderly inspiring the Evangelist. The presence of part of the Sermon on the Mount from Matthew's Gospel on its reverse suggests that this image may once have prefaced the reading for All Saints' Day.

Cap. xii

me ex hac hora: Sed ppterea   ex hora hac.

veni in horam hanc. Pater cla   Sed propterea ve

rifica nomen tuu. Venit ergo   ni in hora hanc.

vox de celo dicens. Et clarifi   Pater illustra no

caui: et iteru clarificabo Turba   men tuum.

ergo que stabat et audierat di   Venit ergo vox

cebat tonitruu esse factum.   de celo, dicens:

Alii autem dicebant. Angelus ei   Et illustraui, et

loquutus est. Respondit IHESVS   rursus illustrabo.

et dixit. Non ppter me hec   Turba ergo que

vox venit: sed ppter vos. Nunc   stabat et audi

iudicium est mundi: Nunc   erat, dicebat

tonitruum esse

factum.

Alii dicebant:

Angelus ei lo

quutus est.

Respondit

sus, et dixit:

Non ppter me hec

vox venit, sed

propter vos.

Nunc iudicium

est mundi huius.

Soon after its completion, the new Latin translation by the Dutch humanist and theologian Erasmus was added in the margins of an earlier copy of the traditional Vulgate text. Both texts were written by the Brabantine scribe Pieter Meghen, who became 'writer of the king's books' under King Henry VIII (1509–47). In the Vulgate text (on the left), the words of God appear in blue, and those of Jesus in red. In the Vulgate the name of Jesus is written in gold, and it is in red in Erasmus's translation.

141 John 12: 27–31, in Latin
New Testament, Vulgate together with the translation of Erasmus
London ?
1509 (Vulgate) and after *c.* 1518 (Erasmus's translation)
450 × 300 mm
Royal MS I E V, Vol. 1, f. 249

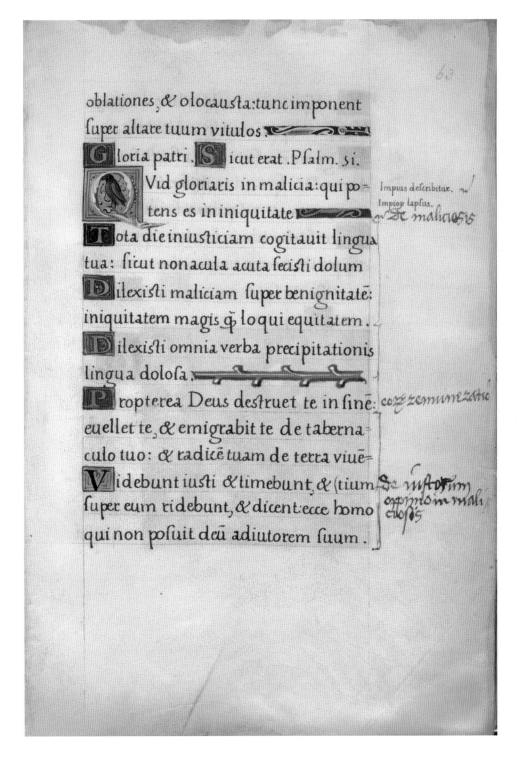

Long after the advent of printed books, lavish copies of Christian scripture continued to be commissioned by wealthy patrons. King Henry VIII's 'orator in the French tongue', Jean Mallard, wrote and illuminated this Psalter for the king in the French style, including portraits of him where earlier copies depicted King David. As indicated by the many marginal notes added in the king's own hand, the volume became the Tudor king's personal copy of the Psalms.

Further Reading

Alexander, J. J. G. (ed.), *A Survey of Manuscripts Illuminated in the British Isles*, 6 vols (London: Harvey Miller, 1975-96)

Backhouse, Janet, *The Illuminated Page: Ten Centuries of Manuscript Painting in the British Library* (London: British Library, 1997)

Brown, Michelle P. (ed.), *In the Beginning: Bibles Before the Year 1000* (Washington: Freer Gallery of Art and Arthur M. Sackler Gallery, 2006)

Brown, Michelle P., *Understanding Illuminated Manuscripts: A Guide to Technical Terms* (London: British Library, 1994)

Cahn, Walter, *Romanesque Bible Illumination* (Ithaca, New York: Cornell University Press, 1982)

The Cambridge History of the Bible, 3 vols (Cambridge: Cambridge University Press, 1963-70)

Cross, F. L. and Livingston, E. A. (eds), *The Oxford Dictionary of the Christian Church*, 3rd edn (Oxford: Oxford University Press, 1997)

de Hamel, Christopher, *The Book: A History of the Bible* (London: Phaidon, 2001)

Fingernagel, Andreas and Gastgeber, Christian (eds), *In the Beginning was the Word: The Power and Glory of Illuminated Bibles* (London: Taschen, 2003)

Gameson, Richard (ed.), *The Early Medieval Bible: Its Production, Decoration and Use* (Cambridge: Cambridge University Press, 1994)

Gibson, Margaret T., *The Bible in the Latin West* (The Medieval Book, vol. 1), (Notre Dame: University of Notre Dame Press, 1993)

Kauffmann, C. M., *Biblical Imagery in Medieval England 700–1500* (London: Harvey Miller, 2003)

Kenyon, Sir Frederic, *Our Bible and the Ancient Manuscripts*, rev. by A. W. Adams, with intro. by G. R. Driver (London: Eyre & Spottiswoode: 1958)

Kenyon, Sir Frederic, *The Story of the Bible: A Popular Account of How It Came to Us*, with chapter by Bernard M. G. Reardon, 2nd edn (London: John Murray, 1964)

Light, Laura, *The Bible in the Twelfth Century: an Exhibition of Manuscripts at the Houghton Library* (Cambridge, MA: Harvard College Library, 1988)

McKendrick, Scot and O'Sullivan, Orlaith (eds), *The Bible as Book: The Transmission of the Greek Text* (London: British Library, 2003)

McKendrick, Scot, *In a Monastery Library: Preserving Codex Sinaiticus and the Greek Written Heritage* (London: British Library, 2006)

Metzger, Bruce M., *Manuscripts of the Greek Bible: An Introduction to Greek Palaeography* (Oxford: Oxford University Press, 1981)

Pattie, T. S., *Manuscripts of the Bible: Greek Bibles in the British Library*, revised edn (London: British Library, 1995)

Sacred: Books of the Three Faiths: Judaism, Christianity, Islam (London: British Library, 2007)

Sharpe, John L. III and Van Kampen, Kimberly (eds), *The Bible as Book: The Manuscript Tradition* (London: British Library, 1998)

Smalley, Beryl, *The Study of the Bible in the Middle Ages*, 3rd edn (Oxford: Blackwell, 1983)

A Thousand Years of the Bible: An Exhibition of Manuscripts from the J. Paul Getty Museum, Malibu, and Printed Books from The Department of Special Collections, University Research Library, UCLA (Malibu: J. Paul Getty Museum, 1991)

Williams, John (ed.), *Imaging the Early Medieval Bible* (University Park: Pennsylvania State University Press, 1999)

For more on illuminated manuscripts in the British Library, see: British Library Catalogue of Illuminated Manuscripts: http://www.bl.uk/catalogues/illuminatedmanuscripts/

Index of Biblical Citations

The Bible chapter numbers cited are to the New International Version,
except for the numbers in brackets, which refer to the Vulgate version.

Index of Manuscripts

General Index

First published 2007 by
The British Library
96 Euston Road
London NW1 2DB

Text © 2007 Scot McKendrick and Kathleen Doyle
Illustrations © 2007 The British Library Board
and other named copyright holders

British Library Cataloguing
in Publication Data
A Catalogue record for this book is
available from The British Library

ISBN 978 0 7123 4922 2

Designed by Andrew Shoolbred
Printed and bound in Italy by Trento S.r.l.

Acknowledgements
The authors would like to thank Jonathan Alexander, François Avril, Colin Baker, Alixe Bovey, Michelle Brown, Richard Gameson, David Ganz, John Lowden, Vrej Nersessian, Katya Rogatchevskaia, Rebecca Rushforth, and Rose Walker for their advice on particular manuscripts included in this book, and in particular Peter Kidd for his helpful comments on various drafts, and Belinda Wilkinson for her careful editing.

2007. 07. 06   35.00   (26.60)